Conflict Resolution for Life

HOW TO RESOLVE ANY
CONFLICTS IN YOUR LIFE

Georgia Lay

Published by
Forward Thinking Publishing

First published 2023

Published by Forward Thinking Publishing

Text © Georgia Lay 2023

The moral rights of the author have been asserted.
All rights reserved. No part of this book may be reproduced by any mechanical, photographic or electronic process, or in the form of a phonographic recording; nor may it be stored in a retrieval system, transmitted or otherwise be copied for public or private use, other than for 'fair use' as brief quotations embodied in articles and reviews, without prior written permission of the publisher.

The information given in this book should not be treated as a substitute for professional medical advice; always consult a medical practitioner. Any use of information in this book is at the reader's discretion and risk. Neither the author nor the publisher can be held responsible for any loss, claim or damage arising out of the use, or misuse, of the suggestions made, the failure to take medical advice or for any material on third party websites.

A catalogue record for this book is available from the British Library.

ISBN: 978-1-7397230-5-7

Contents

Introduction 2
Background 4
Benefits 12
Preparation 30
Position 42
Facts 50
Feelings 65
History Pre-Conflict 72
The Future of the Conflict Area 79
Strengths and Weaknesses 88
Needs and Interests 101
Broader Thinking 112
Best and Worst Alternatives to a Resolution
 118
Broader Aims 126
Thought Process 133
Communication 147
The Advantage of Love 171
Resolution 178

Beyond Resolution 187
Conclusion 193
About the Author.. 195

This book is dedicated to my mother Stavroula Stouppa, who fully understood the power of the written word. Also, in memory of my father, Soterakis, whose own last chapter has just closed before publication.

I would like to thank my husband, Danny who has never failed to back me in all my endeavours, however ambitious or unpredictable. My thanks too to my sons James, Nick and Reuben from whom I have learned so much. I also must thank my friends, who have encouraged me with my projects, especially Suzann and Dave Newton and Dave's sister Kate who, without hesitation and very constructively, agreed to read my initial manuscript. And thank you Ann Hobbs, my Publisher, who has made the publishing process possible and enjoyable.

Introduction

THIS BOOK IS DESIGNED to highlight the real advantages to you of resolving conflicts in your life. We all experience conflict in our personal and working lives, in the form of things not being the way we would like them to be. These conflicts may be over fundamental matters, such as who we are sharing our lives with, what job we do, or where we live. Alternatively, conflicts could constitute anything going on for us at a given time which bothers us because it is not as we wish. This could include internal conflicts such as mental or physical health issues, finance problems, things happening around us or disagreements with those we are close to and even those unconnected to us. All conflicts cause us extra stress, which we would undoubtedly be better off without.

You may have some such obvious disagreements, less obvious concerns or internal anguish about some things not being the way you really want. These issues are conflicts which act to block your life and you will begin to identify and deal with them when reading this book.

To outline a little about myself, I was born in the mid-1960s to Greek Cypriot parents who had settled in London. My upbringing was a traditional Orthodox one, but I was always encouraged in my education. After attending our local comprehensive school, I was one of a few pupils to continue to higher education and I was the first in my immediate family to attend University. Although I studied law, I was not sufficiently self-financing at the time to support qualification and training as a Barrister. I started working life as a Chartered Accountant, working, qualifying, and progressing with one of the big four international firms. Later, having married and started a family of three boys, all now adults, I took the opportunity to re-qualify as a Barrister, and went on to run a Civil and Commercial practice in Bristol Chambers. Due to a chronic neurological condition I retired from practice a few years ago and spent a period concentrating on my health. This led to qualifying and working for a while on a voluntary basis as a yoga/meditation teacher. I returned to the legal arena and gravitated towards mediation, looking at the settlement of legal cases outside court and qualified as a professional mediator. This brought my professional life full circle and into line with my developing ethos and personal thought. I have used my professional and life experience in the management of conflict to write this book.

CHAPTER 1

Background

"If you chew too long it gets bitter"
**An elder of the Raute people, Nepal
- a view on conflict**

CONFLICT RESOLUTION HAS LONG been recognised as a sensible and healthy way forward where frictions arise. The process is a tried and tested method of settling disputes or issues, whether informal or formal conflicts. To begin with I will look back at the history of formal mediation and its dispute resolution forerunners. This is illuminating in relation to striving towards resolution of your life conflicts. You will see how and why the practice began and evolved. I will show you the generally wide and useful applicability of the process, which is testimony to its ability to help you.

History

The origins of mediation are ancient. The far-reaching history of mediation shows how valuable the process has been in very varied settings. Mediation by the Christian Clergy since their establishment, is a Western tradition, while mediation and conciliation have also played a role in most faiths including the Jewish faith, the Islamic culture, and Chinese and other Asian societies. In secular societies too, there has been a worldwide tradition of elders or councils mediating local issues and mediation has traditionally been an integral part of the operation of the social system in the East.

In England, very early on in the development of the Legal System, as early as the Norman Conquest, legal documents indicate that highly regarded members of the lay community were deciding private disputes in informal forums. These decisions would often replace the formal King's Court decisions.

Modern Mediation

The modern mediation process, as an alternative to litigation for dispute resolution, is relatively young with its formal beginnings in early twentieth century America. Today in England and Wales mediation is a required prerequisite to most civil legal claims with cost consequences imposed at trial for parties not attempting a mediated settlement. This was largely established by Lord Wolfe's 1996 reforms to the Civil Procedure Rules, firmly positioning mediation as an accepted and often required step in pre-action protocol. Alternative dispute resolution has also been championed by other legal systems, with Australia for example using it as the primary settlement system, in preference to litigation, and most European countries generally encouraging engagement with the process.

The reason for the existence of dispute resolution alongside and as an alternative to legal systems is mainly that it is well recognised that a non-adversarial, non-competitive approach to problem solving is better all round. It is less stressful to solve a problem than to let it continue and a self-imposed solution which makes sense to the parties and is suggested or agreed by them is so much more wholesome and satisfying than an imposed 'winner' or 'loser'. The time and cost savings are of obvious benefit in comparison to litigation and successful mediation serves to relieve the pressure on overloaded civil legal systems.

The Process

Conflict resolution would traditionally have worked, and indeed does today, by having an objective third party hearing both sides to a dispute and guiding the disagreeing or aggrieved persons, with varying degrees of intervention, but usually with very little substantive input to the final resolution. Because of the usefulness and success of conflict resolution within society, the process has been largely formalised and while still somewhat more of an art than a science, there are steps which can be followed and applied by the individual to address personal conflicts. Of course, sometimes we all reach an impasse and need outside input from a friend, family member, or a professional. However, there is a lot of groundwork to resolving our own conflicts which we can do ourselves, which will sometimes lead to a solution, or at least prepare the way for resolution to occur with a little more help.

With the resolution of conflicts in one's own life a desire to work at the problem and to self-determine is necessary. Attempting to resolve personal conflicts will be disappointing for anyone who is expecting to have an outcome presented to them which is all in their favour without compromise or effort to look at things afresh from an objective viewpoint. Instruction can be taken from the formal mediation process, which is more likely to be successful for all who wish to oversee the resolution of their dispute, exercising their own choice. The process is unlikely to be fruitful for parties who want to be told they are right and are not willing to work hard at achieving a resolution through objectivity and compromise.

The Case for Resolution

In an age where much of the world aspires to moving towards a more peaceful, harmonious and collaborative existence, there is a case for resolving any personal conflicts. Left to fester internal conflicts and disagreements with others tend to eat away at our wellbeing and create stress, which can affect us very negatively. Individual and joint counselling and talking methods of resolving personal issues have increased as popular psychology tools. Meditation and mindfulness have been accepted into mainstream life, in the West as well as Eastern cultures. These practices eliminate stress and create calm enabling full focus on the current moment and the direction in which we wish life to go. In the same way managing conflicts in your life can reduce stress and create clarity and focus for achieving more general fulfilment.

Any conflicts identified in your life can be tackled, whatever stage they are at, from a potential problem to something that has affected you for some time. However, it should be noted that the earlier on you begin the process of identifying and dealing with conflicts, the less ingrained the issues will become, making resolution more attainable and stress more avoidable. Resentment and stubbornness over the issues are less likely to have become entrenched and negative, problem confirming thoughts are less likely to have been engrained as patterns.

A recognition of differences between yourself and others in personal or corporate culture, values, interests, personality, status, or resources can pre-empt disagreements or lead to an agreement to disagree. This can be done by simply having an awareness of the differences which can lead to problems or by timely and thoughtful communication. An impartial person could assist at an early stage to help prevent a dispute, or later at the point when disagreements between parties have caused consequences for at least one party and thereby become a problem. However, you may be just as effective at achieving resolution of differences or problems yourself, armed with the tools employed by professionals. Whether someone else helps or not, the true answers for resolution of conflict will come from *you*.

It is the case that with advanced disagreements, which have perhaps proceeded to initiation of litigation, minds will be focused on the dispute and the emotional and financial risks of perpetuating the problem and maybe proceeding to court. That is why many formal mediations will be arranged after the initial legal steps have been taken and contact with a legal representative has been made. There are many cases which are said to settle 'on the steps of the court' (or a meeting room while the parties await to be called for trial). This is usually because while the parties may be gung-ho and hold their ground on a dispute and issues connected to it in the weeks before trial, when trial becomes a reality and the risks of large monetary loss and a stressful trial are faced, parties are suddenly more willing to compromise. The cutting of losses with the certainty of an agreed settlement becomes a more appealing option to holding out for a risky win. There is a school of thought which favours the progression of disputes to some stage of maturity before attempts at mediated settlements, thereby creating a better environment for successful resolution. However, if a focus of mind and awareness can be created by your input to any conflicts you may have at an early stage, many negative effects on you and your life can be saved.

The stress caused by conflict can lead to a lack of clarity and focus on what is important in your life, blocking the flow of your life in other areas. This can lead to frustration, depression, accidents and illness. You can determine to minimise this by identifying and dealing with conflict in your life now.

Obviously if you have a disagreement or problem with someone else, you cannot guarantee the other side's sentiment in relation to openness and resolution. However, the more work you do to understand the issues fully, the better position you will be in to persuade the other of resolution. At the very least your attitude and emotional response to issues are likely to shift and while that may not achieve total outward resolution, it may well resolve things in your mind and help you to ensure a healthy approach to problems for yourself and a good perspective in life. There are techniques used by professional mediators to encourage resolution; you can use these techniques yourself to manage any conflict in your life. I will be showing you how to do this throughout the book.

Where Resolution is Not Reached

Sometimes a conflict resolution process will not lead to complete resolution, however in those instances the process can still be viewed as a worthwhile exercise, often adding a deeper understanding of issues. As a result of examining a conflict, better communication or mutual appreciation of positions or interests may be established, helping an ongoing relationship or your own peace of mind, despite a specific ongoing issue. This applies equally to the tackling of internal conflicts, even when the problem may be seemingly circumstantial, such as an unwanted injury, illness, event, or situation. The examination of this type of conflict may lead to a resolution if it is something that can be changed by deciding to do so. If it is not in this category, a better understanding of the conflict you are feeling, the origins of your emotions and the reasons behind your thoughts and reactions may lead to living more in harmony with the issue. You may be able to make the changes that you can, which perhaps you had not thought of, accepted, or committed to and these might lead to the problem existing without you feeling so much conflict towards it.

It can be seen from this chapter that a very long and varied system exists of resolving problems through some form of conflict management worldwide, spanning religious and secular traditions in both the Eastern and Western worlds. This acts as testimony to the applicability of the process to resolution of an extremely wide range of issues. The modern adoption and encouragement of mediation, on a national and international basis alongside and within legal systems, endorses the widespread effectiveness of the process across a range of dispute subjects. Just as formal mediation has become accepted and helpful, there will usually be benefit in tackling any personal conflict at least from an increased understanding of the issues and your relationship to them. You will gain from learning the tools of conflict management and using them, whether to tackle conflicts with another or internal ones. You will also be better equipped to spot and deal with a future conflict successfully. Most conflict issues, disagreements and problems, will be suited to management and you will in most instances benefit from this process, if you fully commit to it. In the following chapter I will explain in detail the specific benefits of resolving your conflicts.

CHAPTER 2

Benefits

*"War does not determine who is right
- only who is left"*
Bertrand Russell

THE PROCESS OF CONFLICT resolution involves the thinking through of what has happened to lead to a given problem. It then involves the input of consideration of where you are and where you want to be, in the context of the conflict issue specifically and your life generally. Attempting conflict resolution is far more wholesome than the stress and disruption to your life of continued outward disagreement with another and ongoing internal conflict. Below I will outline why this is and the specific benefits to you of carrying out the exercise and putting the effort into resolution.

Opportunity

Embarking on a conflict resolution exercise is an exciting opportunity, not only to free yourself from a particular entanglement, but also to dispel deeper conflict attached to the issues, which may have hung around on the periphery for a while. Conflicts rarely come to a head in a bubble; they usually arise over time because of individual attitudes and repeated patterns of thought and behaviour. Tackling a problem which seems no longer avoidable may, if investigated in the right way, dissolve deeper personal or joint problems which have never been properly addressed. You or another may be unaware that a particular approach or ingrained way of thinking is contributing to the creation of a problem which might otherwise not have reached an apparent impasse. Not only may past issues be dealt with by tackling a current conflict, but the future may become much less conflict-ridden for you both in the area you are specifically addressing and in wider areas of your life or dealings with others.

Movement Forward in the Conflict Resolution Process

PAST	PRESENT	FUTURE
Beginning of issue	Current Position	Personal aims
(Argument/Internal Conflict)		(Conflict Resolution Process)

The diagram above shows the movement during conflict resolution and the concentration of the process on moving from the present position towards future aims. Argument and internal conflict by contrast is a phase in which one can be shown to dwell on the past origins of a disagreement or problem and move only towards the present, probably involving high stress levels. Unless a decision is made to attempt to resolve the conflict, short of the issue miraculously disappearing, you will not be able to move successfully towards where you would like to be in relation to the issue or in relation to future life aims. If you exist with something which really bothers you, your mind will be affected in terms of detrimental effect on clarity, focus and calm. Even if you argue something through to get your way, a relationship may be left in tatters and considerable emotional or other costs may have been borne by you to 'win' and get your way.

Time will have been diverted to fretting or arguing from other areas of your life and considerable stress may have been caused by the process. None of this, even if you bulldoze through to the solution which you consider ideal, will usually move you closer to your future personal aims. The other risk to arguing is that things might not go your way; in fact, in the acrimony caused by taking the argumentative route, doggedly sticking to your position, things are unlikely to easily yield what you want. So, embarking on a pure argument which leads to a result which you see not to be in your favour, while being just as labour intensive as a good outcome, will aggravate the problem and the anguish for you. This will be more so if, as is usual, time and possibly money, have been expended on the argument.

The conflict resolution process, although based on past facts and a present position, will seek to concentrate upon the movement towards future aims and a resolution arising from a management of conflict process is likely to be in line with that. A successful conflict resolution with an initial investment of time and effort, will certainly see savings in time and stress in the long term, which are factors generally helping to liberate you, restore the flow of your life and achieve future aims. This also undoubtedly represents a saving in cost, which may be financial, as for traditional mediation, but is very likely to be a measurement of lost opportunity, diverted focus, wasted effort and emotional investment all tied up in a conflict, from which you are freed through resolution.

Elimination of Risk

Resolving a conflict will lead to an elimination of risk. Whilst confrontation and arguing your case to its extremes can lead to a change in your situation, there is a risk that you may make the situation worse and be no further forward with your life in general as well as the problem. Furthermore, if you go into headlong battle with someone, they are less likely to see things from your point of view and compromise or find a solution which allows an ongoing relationship. If the turmoil is internal, denial or continued fighting against acceptance of a situation is risky, because if things don't resolve in your favour, you will be worn down by a continued situation. Quite possibly you will have made things worse for yourself, as your wellbeing will suffer from the conflict. Sticking to your guns and marching headlong through a battle of disagreement or non-acceptance causes ongoing uncertainty and pressure, which could be never-ending.

Increased control and autonomy over the conflict area will be within your grasp with a settlement of the issues. An argument with another or a position of resentment towards circumstance will not allow for the exploration of things, other than the immediately obvious, which might have led to the problem. The reasons for a situation or the feelings of another may be overlooked. This problem is avoided during the conflict management process, as there is ample opportunity to consider circumstances surrounding the issue, your viewpoint and that of anyone else involved. Embarking on the process is totally up to you and therefore within your control. No one can tell you anything you don't wish to hear, although you may gently realise for yourself certain truths which help you to move forward. By using conflict management strategies, you can put forward, consider, or dismiss ideas for resolution, which can be of great benefit over the imposition of having to put up with a situation of friction, or another's idea of what should happen. You are empowered to come to a suitable resolution for the disagreement or situation and all its issues for yourself.

The control afforded by the conflict resolution process will serve to reduce your stress. Some of the most stressful situations in life are said to be those where there is no control. Studies have shown that contrary to intuition, it is often not actual pressure which creates stress in a job, but lack of control. The less control an employee has in a job, the more stressful the job is to that employee. Timescales and requirements set rigidly by others cause more stress than self-determined, flexible but maybe very ambitious goals, over which an employee exercises their own autonomy. These findings in the workplace have more general applicability to control and reduced stress generally in life.

The chance to eliminate the risk of a head on confrontation not going your way, or continued anguish over a situation you cannot seem to change, is a stress reliever. If you push an argument, you will be on edge pending the outcome, however sure you are that you are right. By avoiding the build up to and obvious acrimony of argument and non-acceptance you will reduce stress caused by the problem.

The certainty provided by a conflict resolution process which you chose to embark upon and over which you control the conclusion, will bring the possibility of closure and peace of mind, enabling you to move forward with the rest of your personal life. A compromise on the perfect outcome of changing a situation totally to your favour or 'wining' may be conceded with embarking on this process, but you have an immediate chance of things getting better and a reduction in the risk of things going totally against you. The stress attached to the ongoing situation and the risk of things turning against you if left to work themselves out is reduced.

The situation can be likened to the payment of insurance premiums where insurance is voluntary. The payment of the premium will leave the insured in a slightly worse financial position than before he took the policy, but he will be paying to eliminate the risk and stress of a future disaster, which could happen at any time and could cost him much more. There will be a certain payment but an elimination of the stressful risk of losing much more. Equally, mortgagors often chose to fix their mortgage payments at a higher interest rate than the prevalent variable mortgage interest rate, to eliminate the risk and associated stress of the uncertainty brought by relying on a variable rate, which could well go down but might go up.

Stress Reduction

There is privacy in the process of managing a conflict yourself. In embarking on this process, you are not making any public statements or admissions. You can consider the conflict and angles to the issues yourself, which you might not be prepared to voice aloud, or to repeat to anyone. This can be a great benefit to the process and you might find yourself exploring many possible new solutions, in this safe and liberating process. If during the process you consider solutions or viewpoints which you discard after examination, they need not be repeated. If after the process you do not reach an ideal resolution, you will be no worse off and are likely to have gained considerably during it. This privacy is invaluable, as it creates an environment conducive to openness and honesty with yourself, making resolution more likely. It is certainly preferable to take some time to examine a problem fully and privately, than to rant openly or air grievances rashly, probably making a situation worse.

The privacy of resolving a conflict yourself may make you more likely to embark upon the exercise. However, further to this, privacy is connected to control over the situation. When you take control of a problem and decide to act to resolve it, your stress connected to it will begin to reduce. As noted above, it has been suggested that the most stressful jobs are those where there is the most lack of autonomy. It certainly seems that when we think we are trapped by a situation which is dictated to us, we become stressed. Think about a task which needs doing such as clearing out a garage. If you can do this yourself, you will be in control of when and how it is done. You have the choice of leaving it until it suits you, knowing that you will do it the way you want to. The task may hang over you a bit, but it is not highly stressful because you can decide to do it at any point. However, if the job needs to be delegated to someone because you do not have the time or required strength to do it yourself, you start to lose control. If someone has offered to do the job for payment, but continually puts off confirming a time slot, the issue begins to become stressful. It may need to be done but the situation is dictated by another.

In the same way, thinking that a conflict cannot be removed from your life because of circumstance or another, is frustrating, distracting and causes stress. Once you start embarking on the process of thinking about a problem in new ways and finding resolutions you will feel less stress. Of course, once the resolution is achieved and the conflict has been removed from your life there will be a greater saving of stress. One of the greatest benefits of resolving your conflicts will be reduction in the stress which the conflict was creating. Sometimes we are not aware of stress levels and their negative affect on us, until they are removed, and we realise how much better we feel in many ways.

We all thrive on harmony. We tend to be happier and to like ourselves and others more when things are as we wish them to be. Most of us naturally strive to be at peace with ourselves and the way our life is. We generally like others to agree with our viewpoints or to acknowledge our thought processes and decisions. Creating harmony within ourselves and in our relationships and dealings with others is a worthwhile exercise, bringing benefits to our lives. Anyone heading frequently towards acrimony, argument and conflict may be doing so through an actual need to resolve issues.

Time Saving

There will almost certainly be an overall saving of time when a conflict is resolved. You can set aside time to investigate the conflict resolution process and spend time on it as it suits you. Beginning this process improves the quality of the rest of your life by allowing a window for thinking about the conflict. This makes it more likely that you can spend the rest of your time free from thoughts and worries about the issue. Of course, time will need to be spent on the process, but achieving a resolution will be a good time investment as it will then free you totally from being preoccupied with the problem. The sooner you can resolve a problem, the shorter the period of conflict, uncertainty and stress. The more quickly a conflict is dealt with, the more time remains for you to concentrate on the rest of your life. The less protracted a conflict becomes the greater the savings in continued cyclical thought, worrying, arguing and striving fruitlessly for some resolution.

The conflict resolution process may well be achieved in a relatively short time, once you are freed from narrow and cyclical thinking. In formal mediations, especially where parties are sincerely open to achieving a settlement through the process, it is not uncommon to be able to see a settlement in sight within 2 or 3 hours of mediation beginning. This can be so even in a sizeable case where trial would continue beyond a day. The informality of the conflict resolution process means that as soon as you feel you can see a way through a conflict, you can proceed quickly.

Personal Development

Engaging in the conflict management process, there are new skills to be acquired and areas of self-discovery to be explored. If you follow the conflict management strategies set out in this book, your powers of empathy, thinking outside the box, response to others and indeed understanding of yourself will improve. Thinking about things in a fresh way, trying to gain neutrality, calm and resolution may well bring you to consider areas hitherto avoided. This new dynamic will often in itself give rise to new thought processes regarding resolution. Beyond this, you will learn how to explore ways in which a problem causing conflict can be dealt with. Within the theory of conflict resolution, it is accepted that even where a disagreement or problem may have a natural life cycle leading to resolution, intervention may considerably shorten this. In formal mediation, the intervention is by a neutral third party, but the methods used can be employed by you.

Although a conflict may be triggered by external circumstances or actions of another, it may be that your own behaviour in some way serves to exacerbate or perpetuate it. This may happen for many reasons from pride, stubbornness, fear or anger to narrow and protective logic and factual analysis. If you are prepared to be guided to examine your behaviour you may find valuable solutions to issues and resolution of conflict. Of course, you may find yourself examining circumstances or the behaviour of others, which may be undesirable. You have less control over these yourself, but you may gain a deeper understanding of why things have happened, an issue has arisen, or a person has acted in a certain way. This understanding is very valuable, because it can lead to an ability to explain or persuade or to a shift in attitude on your part or that of another. Sometimes outlook can make all the difference. We have all experienced days which seem bleak to us, and others where things are apparently the same but seem bright to us. The difference in the feelings on these days is down to outlook.

Your behaviour and that of any other person involved, which has led to conflict, may stem from a lack of communication, an incorrect viewpoint or a wrong understanding, as pointed out by Acland in "Miscommunication, Misperception, Misunderstanding". This represents a conflict which can be resolved by addressing the underlying deficit. It can be very difficult to discover this deficit on your own, not least because of perpetuating behaviour patterns, but if you are prepared to stand back and employ the methods outlined here, you may be able to pin-point a mismatch in communication, perception or understanding which can resolve an issue relatively simply.

In other situations where there are real differences of opinion, behaviour still serves to perpetuate a dispute. You can help this sort of situation through analysing, trying to break the cyclical thought processes which may have occurred and resolving contributory issues. This can allow you to take a view of a problem which you had not before considered. Although actual opinions may not change, viewpoints in altered contexts often can. There may be differences in background or conflicts in relationship, data, interest, structure or values (as noted by Moore) which led to differing views. While the conflict resolution process may not change your own approach in these areas, it may bring you closer to understanding another's approach, or a turn in circumstance. Agreeing to disagree may be easier when you understand the differences which can exist. With focus and effort, you may be able to break behavioural patterns which are impeding this understanding and so preventing a possible resolution.

Several devices are employed professionally to break an impasse and thereby move closer to resolution. These devices can teach us much in themselves. One such device is brainstorming. Take this fairly well-known problem-solving technique as an example, which will be explored in more detail later. All possible ideas for solutions are recorded without complicating them by considering their merit further, initially. This establishes a creative flow of a variety of ideas, often giving rise to a useful gem, hidden among them. You could brainstorm in your current mode of thinking and come up with useful solutions. However, it is the consideration of ideas from other viewpoints and developing a more objective approach to examining the ideas which can lead to a successful brainstorming session, actually likely to give rise to points which could truly lead to resolution. The ideas from brainstorming often need further consideration and exploration as they are by nature, embryonic. You can work on creating a good opportunity for this to happen constructively by taking a fresh approach to mulling things over and using the guidance of this book to lead you in a different direction.

Preserving Relationships

Through resolving conflicts, relationships can be salvaged and enhanced. A successful resolution of an argument with another will have the advantage of the best chances of establishing or preserving a harmonious relationship between the persons concerned. Since conflict resolution is seen to be a 'win-win' situation, with a compromised but acceptable solution, it is likely that you will regain good terms with anyone else involved.

In the case of internal conflict, having gone through this alternative thought process, you may like yourself or your situation a little more, which helps with finding peace and positive progression. As noted above the relationship may be improved going forward with the conflict management process even where a successful resolution is not reached. However, where the process is successful, relations are likely to have improved and the path for a good ongoing relationship will be established. If a disagreement is left to continue, those involved may never speak to each other again after the acrimony created. Anyone concerned may feel bitter about wasted time and stress, while also feeling alienated and resentful. By contrast, conflict management will require examination and exploration of issues surrounding the facts. It is difficult to partake in all of this and to come to ideas for resolution without feeling some purpose and understanding of the flip side of the conflict.

Most of the above benefits are fairly general. There will often be additional specific benefits to resolving a conflict. There may be important opportunities which are open to you directly due to eliminating the conflict, which may have been closed to you otherwise. It is a good driving force for successful resolution to identify and appreciate the threats posed to you by this particular conflict and the opportunities which would be released through resolution.

Ask These Questions

- Are there other ventures which could come out of a relationship which is in current gridlock?
- May there be knock-on effects of resolution to other areas peripheral to the conflict?

This is a good stage at which to consider these more specific benefits of the conflict resolution, as well as the more general ones. Fully appreciating all beneficial aspects of resolution at the outset of this exercise can provide positive enthusiasm for the process and impetus for success.

Creativity

Through conflict management, creativity will usually occur. It may be tempting to think that if you hold all the answers to the problem and a resolution is coming only from you, that conflict management cannot add value. However, one only has to consider the thought process of great philosophers; philosophical breakthroughs were always within them, but it took a trigger to bring about that thought. Historical stories have it that it took an apple falling on Newton's head for him to discover gravity and an overflowing bath for Archimedes to discover buoyancy. These stories may well have been embellished, but they serve to illustrate that a trigger can cause a different use of the knowledge that you have or a different way of viewing a problem. The conflict management process can trigger such changes.

The ideas and solutions which arise from the process of conflict resolution can be as creative as you wish them to be. This is a totally flexible process, and any solution is possible. The process can take the place of viewing things narrowly and addressing only part of a wider problem which exists between people or within yourself. Deeper or peripheral problems are usually not immediately obvious to us, and while things may sometimes seem to sort themselves out, unresolved issues may remain. Rather than sticking to entrenched views, the conflict resolution process acts as a forum to fully explore past, present and future. So, while a resolution arising from this may take any form acceptable to you, allowing greater flexibility and creativity to be applied to the problem may also air wider grievances or issues, making them part of the solution.

There is a benefit to managing a conflict in an informal manner. Through this process, although there is a usual structure, you will be free to explore and acknowledge your emotions and thoughts, which may have been overlooked by regarding an argument or situation simplistically, or at face value. In fact, you are encouraged to 'vent' emotions during the process; this is part of moving past an emotional position, towards needs and interests, which may lead closer to resolution of issues. You are the only observer in this particular process so you can embrace honesty and let your thoughts rage. Allowing yourself and encouraging from yourself this freedom of thought expression can naturally lead to uncovering the true causes of a problem. Very often such causes can remain hidden and ongoing if things are allowed to take their course without your intervention and pause for honest thought.

Finality

There will be finality to a conflict situation by reaching a successful conclusion to this exercise. A resolution will usually signify the real end to both an argument or internal turmoil and any underlying conflict. Left alone problems may resolve but the original causes of a problem may go unresolved, and you are open to there being likely continued issues. So, conflict resolution can provide finality to problems in ways seldom achieved by letting things sort themselves out.

There are even benefits of a conflict management with no resolution. It should be stressed that if you attempt conflict resolution which does not culminate in an envisaged resolution, there will undoubtedly have been benefits to you, regarding the issues and in general. It is also the case that a problem which has led to the conflict management process may have yielded the advantage of also leading to salvaging some relationship with another or improved self-understanding. Through examination and deeper appreciation of situations we often gain some acceptance. It is difficult to think logically, objectively and broadly about a grievance without some empathy, sympathy and understanding for the situation, even if a suitable resolution cannot be reached. All is not necessarily lost if the process itself does not end in an acceptable resolution; you are in no worse a position in terms of the outcome of the problem. It may be that the problematic issues have been narrowed, thereby gaining something through engagement in the process. So, the time spent will not automatically be wasted if envisaged resolution is not reached.

This is not to say that the process should be suggested or entered into with a half-hearted attitude. Anyone with the intention of conceding nothing and fixated upon having things their way is taking the wrong approach to conflict resolution and as a result missing a real opportunity to swap a resolution for a lengthy, stressful and in many ways, a possibly costly journey which always has the potential to end disastrously.

Letting conflicts with another or internal conflict continue is risky and stressful, precluding your control in many ways. The conflict resolution process is advantageous because it can eliminate this risk and restore control, reduce stress and redirect valuable time thus restoring harmony to your life. Taking direct control and responsibility for one's own issues in life, deciding to deal with conflict yourself and finding resolutions, will enable you to move towards individual future life goals. A resolution can be flexible and creative and may cover issues beyond those immediately obvious.

Even where you think there is no way forward for a situation, the conflict resolution process can lead to creativity and realisations which end the conflict. These can not only be about the issues considered but also about yourself, ongoing relationships and patterns of thought and behaviour. The conflict management process which you carry out yourself is unlikely to have any negative effects on a problem, so there is nothing to be lost. An added bonus of the process is not only learning a new skill but also what you will personally learn about yourself, when you consider things objectively and from fresh angles. Now you have seen the reasons to go forward with the exercise of resolution, your intentions will be positive from the outset. In the next chapter I will explain how to prepare yourself and your surroundings for the exercise mentally, to create the best chance of the most success.

CHAPTER 3

Preparation

"Knowing yourself is the beginning of all wisdom"
Aristotle

PLANNING THE CONFLICT RESOLUTION process and thinking about how you will approach it and make time and space for it in your life will create a solid starting point for success. Below I will take you through the aspects of yourself mentally and physically, which you should consider before starting to think about your conflicts and the practical preparations which will help. You may even find that a good side effect of this planning will be greater organisation within your life generally and an increased awareness of the areas in your personality which you consider require more concentration. It is certainly an exercise which is likely to lead to increased self-awareness, as are most new processes to which we turn our minds.

Strengths and Weaknesses

The best starting point for any work on conflict resolution which you plan to do is to know your own strengths and weaknesses. Consider the way you individually think and approach things and your own tendencies. It is important to recognise personal traits which should assist you and those which could hamper the process. This is a type of analysis on yourself which you may not always have carried out and fed back to yourself. It is however a very ancient, tried and tested means of self-management and ensuring that thought processes lead to the right conclusions. I will explain a bit more about how to start this analysis with questions you can consider.

Do you know what your personality strengths and weaknesses are? Look at the thought pattern and interpersonal skill strengths and weaknesses which you know about yourself, generally accept and reveal to others. Also look at the strengths and weaknesses which others generally recognise in you and often identify, or those which have been mentioned to you by the people who know you well.

For example:
- Do you consider yourself a logical step-by-step thinker?
- Do you have a more broad-brush approach?
- Are you a good listener or do you prefer to do the talking?
- Are you quick to admit mistakes or more defensive?
- Do you hold grudges or are you more forgiving?

Try to assess yourself honestly, listing any skills you are particularly good or bad at, which immediately come to mind.

Delve into those traits which you know about but are reluctant to admit and tend to hide from others. Look even for those traits which are usually hidden both from yourself and others; you may only recognise or accept these after specific thought on the subject. You may have to survey your thoughts and actions in other situations in life or examine more deeply than usual the reactions and responses to you from others, to identify this category of your strengths and weaknesses.

The reason for identifying your strengths and weaknesses is so that you can use your strengths and compensate for your weaknesses. If you know that you are not a step-by-step thinker, maybe make a list of thoughts, to check your logic before jumping ahead. If you know memory is not your strong point, you could have conversations to clarify past facts relating to a conflict or make extra effort to recall and record issues surrounding a problem.

If you know you are slow to see things from the perspective of others, make an extra effort to be objective when the time comes for that. If you are someone who responds better to pictorial representation of things, rather than words, make diagrams as opposed to lists. You may feel that you are not sure where to start with this, but you should not be concerned. You probably know yourself quite well and have these answers if you spend a bit of time thinking about it. Give yourself a chance to think about this now, with some suggested areas for thought below, and simply be aware of your conclusions.

Awareness is the most important step to change or improvement, so there is no need to force yourself to suddenly change your approach. You may realise a trait in yourself which you wish to improve and that will start to happen just from the awareness of it. When the time comes to carry out each step described in this book, simply be aware of your personal skills in that area. Think about what you should spend more time on, to suit your weaknesses and methods which will help you with the process, such as writing things down, or drawing diagrams.

Maybe your weakness is lack of empathy, or objectivity more generally, the importance of which is covered below. You may need to make special efforts to work on this aspect of yourself to reach good decisions on a conflict. Conversely you might find it more difficult to put yourself first, therefore blocking decisions leading to resolution which is truly workable for you. You may wish to work on such weaknesses in yourself which you recognise, within your everyday life, alongside the exercise of moving towards resolving conflict. This may sound understandably daunting, but once you have identified and named your weaknesses you will be more likely to notice when they come up and be able to adjust yourself.

Much of the thought involved in the stages outlined below will bring out aspects of self-discovery and growth which should be encouraged as part of this process, both for their own sake and as a greater insurance of success in reaching a harmonious resolution. Of course, this will take time, effort and honesty, but the input will be worthwhile. If you feel unable to assess yourself or your strengths and weaknesses in managing tasks and making decisions, maybe ask a trusted friend or family member to give you an opinion, if you are prepared to do so without falling into a further conflict.

How Do You View Things?

How you view things will give you an insight into how you approach the conflict process. Some categories of tendencies to consider are procrastination, confidence, optimism/ pessimism, tenacity and distraction – these are expanded on below. You may think of other areas of strength or weakness to include. Try to consider the way you look at things and whether others you know generally view things differently. The theory of those who understand their own methods of observation has been outlined by H. Von Foerster and N. Luhmann. Look at the differences in viewpoints in all sorts of areas other than the conflict and the reasons for the differences. This is about becoming the type of observer who is aware of how they observe. Becoming this type of observer will help you to learn from mistakes. Changes to conflict situations can come about from reassessing our viewpoints. This is not about capitulating to the other standpoint in a conflict; it is about understanding our own reasons for thought and actions and our own aims. An understanding in this area can give rise to real shifts in areas otherwise blocked.

Procrastination

Some of us are prone to procrastination. That may be delaying getting down to starting something, or it may be delaying the completion of something. If you recognise this in yourself, you will have to exercise high levels of self-discipline to embark on the decision-making task and/or in order to stay on track and effectively complete the task. Procrastination tends to be influenced by how long we think something will take, how distracted we are, how much confidence we have in success at the task and the value we see in the task. So, give some thought to these areas and be aware of putting things off if that might or does start to happen. It is particularly difficult to avoid delaying if you are prone to it and are embarking on this exercise alone. Mediators often help in reaching resolution by scheduling the process and keeping it on track. This is a job you will have to manage. Ensure you have set aside time for decision-making and the other stages in this book, so that they happen and be aware of seeing them through. Give yourself set times for work on resolution, with realistic deadlines if you will need them. Be stricter with your schedule if you recognise that you may have a tendency to avoid the work.

Self-Confidence

It may be that self-confidence is an area in which you struggle. Self-confidence is important within this process because it is helpful to be positive about your thoughts and to trust that acting upon your realisations will improve things. If you recognise a lack of trust in your intuition or thoughts, you should be aware of the impact on this exercise and try to approach things with as positive a mind-set as possible. Of course, it is not easy to upgrade your personality overnight for the purposes of settling a conflict, but you may be able to watch out for negativity. If, and when you reach dead ends in your thinking or management of the conflict, instead of believing that there is no way forward, try to see this juncture as a minor setback in the process and not an automatic failure of it. When you have thoughts and realisations about the conflict area, be aware of trusting that these are valid.

Are You Optimistic or Pessimistic?

Whether you are optimistic or pessimistic by nature is also relevant to the conflict resolution exercise you are undertaking. If you know you are an optimist, you should consciously allow yourself to look into the future to consider how your decisions could affect things negatively. Optimists are naturally less likely to do this, as they will typically assume positive outcomes. Conversely if you are a pessimist by nature, you will be used to looking ahead and seeing pitfalls, but do not dwell on these or allow them to stop a decision being made. Either way you should not be afraid to look for things which could go wrong, but do not assume that they will.

Generally, positivity is a good way to approach this exercise. Try to accept new ideas which occur during the process and avoid the internal responses of 'No!', 'But...' or the launching into an internal argument with a myriad of reasons against an idea. It is better to start the process with an accepting and expansive approach to new ideas. Be prepared to be interested in your own wider thought, rather than dismissive or defeatist about ideas.

Tenacity

An extension of optimism is tenacity. Be prepared to not be easily put off the exercise by some initial ideas seeming unworkable. It is not realistic to assume that 100% of the time spent on conflict resolution will be productive and yield solutions. This does not however mean that time has been wasted. The effort is cumulative and at any point in the exercise just a little more concentration could make the difference between having and losing a problem. Try not to feel hopeless for resolution because it does not occur immediately, or because the direction of resolution does not seem clear. This is where following the format set out in this book and the suggested steps to resolution can help to create a positive feeling of keeping on task.

Minimise External and Internal Distractions

Are you easily distracted? We all require certain conditions to focus, but we all vary slightly. For example, some people can concentrate better with music or background sound and others require total silence. Consider this in deciding when and where you will carry out the resolution work. Here you will start to think about the right physical surroundings for the exercise, including some more considerations below. You should minimise both external and internal distractions because multi-tasking as an effective way of running any exercise is illusory. We are better and more efficient when we focus and you should therefore ensure that your attention is not diverted or divided by anything other than resolution of the conflict, for the time spent on this exercise. There are several things which you can manage to promote focus.

You should also minimise internal distractions by creating a good focus on the resolution work and an atmosphere of personal challenge at the right level for you. To explain this further, our minds tend to work best when tuned in to something which challenges us and matches our skill level. This is the reason why people find hobbies fulfilling. Doing something which we enjoy, and which provides a challenge to our skill level so as not to bore us, makes for a productive and efficient state. We become energised by the focus, rather than tired by it and are less likely to be fatigued by distractions. You can create this atmosphere by choosing to engage in a hobby, or something which interests you providing stimulation which you also enjoy, immediately before spending time on the conflict resolution exercise. You can increase internal focus during the exercise by writing things down, which concentrates the mind, leaving less room for distracting thoughts.

Time and space are practical things which you can consider in order to create an atmosphere conducive to a successful resolution of your issues. It will be difficult to carry out new thinking and the exercises suggested here without putting aside set time for this. It would be sensible to set aside a chunk of time on a daily or weekly basis, which is dedicated to conflict resolution.

By doing this you will not be constantly hassled by the need to get on with resolution; the time to devote to this will be pre-allocated. You should not be hassled by other work or life tasks which require your time, as a break from and a return to these will have been set out. In allowing proper allocated time for resolution, you should be able to afford yourself the opportunity to read the techniques set out here and to apply them, both through time for logical review and thought and time for more creative thought. Creative thought tends to happen during or after rest periods or over a period of time, so the process of resolution and the time devoted to it should not be rushed. Space allocated to resolution is important in that you should have a quiet place to work on this where you will not fear interruption or being watched in the process, which you may rightly see as a private matter. You should feel comfortable wherever you chose to begin this work and if possible, your surroundings should be neutral to the issues. For example, if the conflict is over a house in which you are living, try to resolve the issue away from that house, where you will not be reminded of the contentious issues and irritated by them, causing a return to old patterns of thinking.

Rest

It is important to remember that when using the brain to sift through information and then to analyse by comparison to norms and life experience, there is a constant switching of brain functions from memory to analysis which is tiring. Rest can bring clarity. When making decisions, allow yourself to have a break from the thinking if it is causing fatigue. A night's sleep or even a power nap can give the brain enough rest to allow a clear perspective. The benefits of allowing intuitive and subconscious involvement in decision-making will be further discussed.

You should allow for the fact that sleep enables both conscious and unconscious thoughts to be connected, so the rest helps the logic, as well as the out-of-box ideas. Try to get enough good quality sleep before and around the time you will be devoting to considering resolution of your conflict issues and ensure you are well rested generally. During the process, even a short nap can create a more positive outlook and enhance cognitive ability. Do not shy away from taking a rest during resolution time, by doing something restful or sleeping. This may include stopping the exercise for a short time or for some longer time and perhaps not resuming until you have had a good night's sleep. Be aware of mental and physical fatigue and how these can ambush the resolution process for you.

Physical and Mental

Exercise and good eating are also well known to create conditions conducive to getting the most from yourself mentally. Do not put either fresh air and exercise, or proper healthy eating on hold for the purposes of fitting in and completing the resolution exercise. You may think you are buying time by skipping a meal, a lunchtime walk, or a morning gym session, but this could be counterproductive, in terms of operating clearly and efficiently and therefore finding a successful resolution.

In addition to being aware of your own strengths and weaknesses, good mental preparation will be to fully appreciate the benefits to you of the resolution exercise, set out in the last chapter. This will create a positive attitude and you can then allow your focus on an intention to resolve your conflicts. Intention, as mentioned above, is an important element in successful resolution. If you begin this exercise with a positive intention to succeed in resolution, for the right reasons, you will be in the best mental state to achieve this.

Taking time to consider your personal strengths and weaknesses will reinforce what you already know of yourself and add another dimension to that knowledge. Awareness of how you operate, think and respond to situations and others will help you to achieve success in the work of resolving your conflicts. Providing the right environment, space and time for the process will also be preparation which will lead to greater success. So too will be ensuring your own best mental and physical state when you carry out the work. Once you have made these preparations, you will be ready to start thinking about your current position on a conflict, which is the topic I deal with next.

CHAPTER 4

Position

"To reconcile conflicting parties we must have the ability to understand the suffering of both sides"
Thich Nhat Hanh

CLARIFYING YOUR POSITION IS a good starting point for a personal conflict management exercise, helping to focus your mind on the conflict you are tackling, the effects on you and your current position. It is useful to summarise the conflict from your viewpoint and record your own starting position and here I will show you how to do this. This is also an opportunity to identify anything in your life creating conflict, of which you may not have been fully aware before. If you identify more than one conflict, you can deal with just one at this stage and for the following stages of the resolution exercise and come back to others later to repeat the whole exercise.

Formal Position Statement

Participants in a formal mediation are asked to prepare a Position Statement for the purposes of a background starting point and opening the session. This is ideally a document of no more than 5-6 pages, presenting a snapshot of the situation as it stands, completed by each participant. It is an opportunity for the parties to explain the situation they are currently in, regarding the conflict. They will be encouraged to explain how things are and how they feel now, what has been the effect and cost of the conflict to them and what they hope to achieve or gain from mediation, together with any important points they wish to make. Clarifying and fully understanding one's own position is important. Parties should appreciate the specific negative effects on themselves of the conflict and therefore what they initially and ideally require from mediation. It will be confusing to try to examine a conflict further, to understand another's position, or to work towards resolution without fully knowing and stating your own position first. This is the theory behind the informal notes you will make now on your position on a given conflict.

The Facts

The facts do not need to be fully comprehensively recorded now, as that will be covered in the next stage of the exercise. Neither does any exact current idea of realistic resolution need to be decided upon or included, as that will hopefully arise out of the process. The statement in this exercise can be a page of bullet point notes, which is useful to start from and clear to refer back to. If you wish to stop at this, it will be sufficient. If, however, you find it helpful to expand upon this and produce a longer expression of your standpoint, that can be useful too, both in terms of emotional output and as a full record to come back to.

When preparing to set out your position, it is important that you consider the main relevant facts. It is usual to begin with non-contentious facts, which are agreed about the nature of the problem. You can then move on to points over which there is disagreement, listing your points and reasoning and any opposing points which you may list explaining whether and why you accept, question or reject them at this stage. Whilst you are highlighting disagreements here, it is not the time to start attempting to justify your case or criticise the situation. Set out your differences as plainly as possible. Position documents can highlight differences in understanding of the fundamental parts of a conflict and where this happens there is a good starting point for resolution examination.

Issues Important to You

If there are issues which you think are particularly important, they should be flagged, so that there can be focus on this from the start. You can include central issues of importance but also anything less obviously connected which is still of importance to you, in relation to the conflict. Start the conflict management process prepared to consider any important peripheral issues. Search for them now, acknowledge them to yourself and think about how they affect your approach to this conflict. The identification of important issues from your perspective will help to shape the conflict management process, keep it on track and send it in a direction which is useful and meaningful to you.

Costs

In a formal mediation actual financial costs are set out at this point. For this exercise, as well as outlining the bones of the conflict, how far it has progressed and the central or important issues, the statement should also include a summary of actual and emotional or other costs to you. From there you should state what it would take to compensate for the negative effects on you so far and to adjust the position in line with your ideal situation. Knowing all the 'losses' to you of a conflict and what you want now clarifies your starting point and helps to define an upper limit of your envisaged resolution. This figure or list will not generally need to be precise at this stage, but it is useful to have an idea of it before beginning the conflict resolution, for your own information.

Of course, it may be possible that you already have some realistic, compromised level of resolution in mind or concessions you would be happy with under set conditions. Sometimes this is recorded privately at the beginning of a formal mediation. You could do the same, by separately dealing with this if you are advanced to that position and keeping a record for yourself only, to which you can refer later. The full conflict management exercise is still relevant and changes to your current position are the possibility of the process.

Example Position Points Records

It may be helpful for clarity to introduce three basic, fictional problems for the purposes of illustration, which will be used throughout the book, at each stage of the exercise. These are the problems to be used:

1. Conflict on where to live (relationship conflict).
2. Conflict over serious injury (internal/situational conflict).
3. Conflict over job (work life conflict).

The examples are included throughout this book to illustrate each part of the conflict management exercise described, in practical operation, relating to fictitious and general examples.

An example bulleted position record for each of the three listed conflicts is included below. These are of course not suggested statement points for you, even if your conflict is in a similar area, because the points for your conflict will be specific to you:

Conflict on Where to Live
- Two years of arguments over where to live
- Preference has always been for the country
- Preference of partner is town
- Have lived in town for five years
- Have compromised on preference of living in the country
- Cost of reduced wellbeing
- Cost of family missing out on the pleasure/experience of nature
- Cost to relationship of continued conflict
- Children should be brought up surrounded by nature
- Recognition of benefit to partner of being near work

- Would like to sell town house and move to the country
- Would like to reserve funds from sale for family break to strengthen relationship/provide new experience for children

[I would be happy to concede a new car from sales funds for my partner who will have more travel time.]

Conflict over Serious Injury
- Serious injury affecting mobility
- Has affected close relationships
- Has limited social life
- Has curtailed leisure travel and events
- Has impacted on hobbies
- Has interfered with work life
- Has blocked plans for the future
- Would like to live as well as possible with the injury
- Would like an acceptable balance of all the above in life
- Willing to make changes in life

[May be willing to give up a major affected area if the benefits are great enough.]

Conflict Involving Your Job
- Passed over for promotion
- Hard work not recognised
- Loyalty to company not acknowledged
- No reasoning for promotion going elsewhere
- Has prevented a salary rise
- Has created an atmosphere of resentment

- Has left a feeling of being undervalued
- Would like a discussion and reasoning
- Would like reassurance of value to company
- Would like to achieve promotion
- Would like a salary rise

[Would concede immediate promotion and be willing to attain a promotion and salary raise over a set time if agreed.]

Objectivity

At a later stage in the resolution exercise, you will need to be prepared to begin to reality test the level of the strengths you see in your position and the likelihood of your best resolution scenario occurring.

It can be useful when you get to that stage to attempt to produce a record of the starting position from another's point of view, or from outside your internal view of a situation. It might be that you can explain the idea of the statement to a person with whom you are in conflict, when you are ready, so that they can state their own position as a starting point for discussion. If this is the case, it is still useful to have attempted the exercise of what their position might be at this point, as preparation for communication. At this stage, however, producing a record of your own position is the aim and the idea of an opposite statement will be revisited further into the exercise.

The summary you produce will naturally show how right you think you are. From now on though, you should attempt to be as objective as possible. This includes not only reality testing later on, but also the very next stage from where you are now, which is the full collation of facts surrounding the conflict, even those which are not of obvious importance or relevance to you or do not clearly support your position. The next stage of work will be to make a record of all the facts of the situation of and surrounding the conflict and I deal with that in the following chapter.

CHAPTER 5

Facts

"You never really understand a person until you consider things from his point of view"
Harper Lee

IN SOME CASES, THERE will be a written version of the facts to a dispute; where letters have been exchanged or meetings have been recorded. In the case of internal conflicts, a journal charting events and emotions may have been kept. These written records are useful to look back over to review the salient facts of the situation and their ramifications. This is good as part of the starting point in your conflict resolution exercise. It is an advantage if a record already exists as you will be able to review it in the light of your current attitude to the situation. This very exercise might throw up differences between a past attitude and current thinking. Some thoughts might have developed or been diluted over time. Take a look at the record you have, take time to consider any further facts which may be relevant to the issues surrounding the problem or any potential resolution. These may be facts not directly connected to a conflict, on the face of it. The process of information gathering, fact finding, and fact recording is examined below.

Information Gathering

If a written record is not available, care must be taken to collate all facts relevant to the situation, as one of the initial steps to conflict resolution. As part of this exercise record the obvious facts and then extend your fact examination to periphery issues, maybe not considered as connected before. It will be important to being objective and to starting to view things from the opposite standpoint, to include facts relevant to another as well as to you.

When lawyers and mediators are taught to gather information from someone about an issue, they are instructed to ask open, non-leading questions and to drill down to further detail. Open questions, which do not 'lead' are asked to keep an account of a situation full, truthful, and uninfluenced by other factors such as presumptions, or questions which put a suggestion of something into someone's mind. To illustrate this, the question "Can you tell me what happened?" is an open question which requires an explanation answer.

Questions asking who, what, when, why, where, and how are usually open and cannot be answered with a yes or no. The above question is also non-leading as it infers only an accepted fact which is that something happened. Conversely, the question "The man hurt you, didn't he?" is a closed question which requires a yes or no answer and it is also a leading question implying that the man did hurt you and encouraging a yes answer. Try to ask yourself open questions which encourage you to examine the account of a situation afresh in a full way. Try to also imagine what another onlooker's account of the situation might be if asked. Although you are asking yourself questions and cannot limit or mislead yourself in the same way as a questioner can another person, it is important to avoid making assumptions or following an established or narrow way of thinking about an issue. Leave the way open to new thought and resolution through not automatically returning to well-trodden paths.

Drilling down to further detail is a technique designed to capture all facts about an issue. To put this into operation, an open question is usually followed by trying to find out more about the things mentioned. Try to follow through your own fresh account of the situation in order to record as many points at each stage as you can. You may find that there are details which you have not considered before or have glossed over. Every time you identify a strand of the account of the issue, examine any details you can think of which flow from that. Examine the situation as slowly, methodically, and thoroughly as you can, trying to concentrate on finding details about facts you might not have taken note of before. Include all connected details which you can think of, not stopping at this stage to examine their degree of relevance. Trying to filter details for relevance to resolution at this early stage will hamper your free-flowing collation of information and recording of fact and detail. It will also deflect your mind from the task of full information gathering and fact finding. Memory and analysis are different brain functions; attempting to assess facts too strongly now will cause your brain to switch to an analytical mode. You need your brain to be mainly in recall mode currently in order to effectively complete the initial stage of gathering fact and detail. Just as the body becomes overwhelmed by too much multi-tasking, so too does the brain if asked to analyse as well as searching, basic sorting and remembering.

You may have a relationship with the other party which has been affected by other events, known to both of you. There may be actions of the other party outside this dispute which have affected your approach to this conflict, which may or may not have been acknowledged by the other party or discussed. There may be certain of your own actions in different areas which you think should be further explained to the other party. There may be things you wish to know more about which are not directly or obviously part of a conflict but are important to you in resolving this problem. Think about these aspects in order to include less obvious but relevant facts.

What We Know

There is a model of things which we know and things which we do not know, each falling into the categories of known and unknown things, which was an idea put forward by Donald Rumsfeld, US Secretary of Defence under George W. Bush in 2002. When considering facts, it may help to take into account that there are things which we know about, both which we realise we know (known knowns) and which we do not realise that we know (unknown knowns). There are other facts which we do not know about, which equally we may be aware of on some level (unknown knowns) or not aware of at all (unknown unknowns).

Sometimes things that we do not know about are relevant. As mentioned, they can either be attainable from somewhere in our subconscious if they are known on some level, or they can be accessed by research and wider thought if they are totally unknown. Take as an example the weather over two spring days in the UK. If we can see that it is sunny today, we can say that we know the weather today, but we do not know the weather tomorrow. In other words, the sunny weather today is a fact which we know that we know. The weather tomorrow is a fact which we know that we do not know.

In considering the weather tomorrow we may list as relevant facts the information that it is spring, and it has been sunny today. From this our thoughts may logically lead us to the other possible weather conditions for the time of year, following a sunny day and we may consider cloud or rain as well as sun. However, it could actually snow. We might have known this from past experience or from information we know about past weather at that time of year. In this case the fact that it could snow tomorrow is a fact which we know but have not considered, may be due to it being so rare as to seem irrelevant. Therefore, it is an unknown fact for the purposes of the exercise but actually known.

Discovering facts such as these often depends upon the use of intuition. It is necessary to start feeling about the subject as well as applying logical thought. In the example of weather conditions for the next day, the possibility of snow could occur to us if we start to tune in to the temperature and realise that although it is sunny today, it is unseasonably cold. Alternatively, we might not be aware that it could snow in spring because we may never have experienced it, due to it not occurring in our lifetime or maybe due to our being out of the country on the rare occasions when this might have happened. In that case it is a fact which we do not know that we don't know about. This unknown fact can be more readily discovered through wider thought and research.

Once again, intuition and tuning in to feeling will help to start the thought process in the direction of unknown unknowns. If we realise that it feels unseasonably cold, despite the sun today, it may prompt us to research past weather conditions in spring going back beyond our memory or outside our direct experience. We might then find a relevant fact which should be included in our assessment, which we did not know of. Considering these two types of unknown facts and attempting to identify and include them can be useful at the information gathering stage of this exercise and again when we come to expand our thoughts around the conflict and possible solutions.

Recording Facts

Thinking about relevant facts as a starting point, will ensure that there is full information for you to examine in relation to what is important to you. Putting some time into thinking about this and making notes without any pressure of reaction to your thoughts from outside, or any pressure to find a solution, will make you less likely to forget to include facts in your further examination. This will be the foundation to your work on resolution and the more solid and complete this stage is, the more chance of an examination broad enough to lead to a successful resolution. Full facts will ensure that you make good use of the time you spend managing the conflict. Use the following table to record facts which may be relevant to provide, discover or consider during the process.

Accepted Facts
Contentious Facts
Facts of previous history
Historical facts outside the conflict

Relationship issues of importance to you

Emotional issues of importance to you

Facts requiring clarification

Facts you can uncover needing further discovery

Facts required from another

Facts peripheral to the problem

Here are three examples of initial fact recordings for conflicts, repeating the examples already referred to:

1. Conflict on Where to Live

Accepted Facts
Argument about where to live Country v Town
Contentious Facts
Costs Work Children
Facts of previous history
Communication issues Arguments around finances Independence issues over work Anxiety over your children's reactions
Historical facts outside the conflict
Family backgrounds Personal aspirations Work ambitions Past understandings/agreements over the above

Relationship issues of importance to you Staying together Improving communication Feeling personally fulfilled
Emotional issues of importance to you Mutual happiness Personal mental health
Facts requiring clarification Is this an either/or choice? Are there further options?
Facts you can uncover needing further discovery Your limits for compromise Further reasons behind your preference
Facts required from another Acceptable alternatives Possible compromises

Facts peripheral to the problem
Opinions of others
Parenting issues

2. Conflict over Serious Injury

Accepted Facts
Serious injury
Physical/ mental symptoms
Interference with family life
Interference with work life
Concern for future

Contentious Facts
Effect on marriage
Emotional effect
Interaction with your personality

Facts of previous history
Few previous setbacks
Mind-set of achiever

Historical facts outside the conflict Attitude to others with injury Stress coping mechanisms Functioning at unsustainable level
Relationship issues of importance to you Self-acceptance Personal fulfilment Excitement for the future
Emotional issues of importance to you Happiness Energy and vitality Achievement
Facts requiring clarification Treatment available More information on recovery
Facts you can uncover needing further discovery Medical facts

Facts required from another Attitude of family members
Facts peripheral to the problem Unequal workload in the family Reliance of others on you Support giver role not receiver

3. Conflict Involving Work

Accepted Facts Promotion at work denied
Contentious Facts Reasons for denial
Facts of previous history No system for voicing your needs at work

Historical facts outside the conflict Organisation problems with employee turnover
Relationship issues of importance to you Loyalty to organisation Bonds with colleagues
Emotional issues of importance to you Work/life balance Achievement at work Personal growth
Facts requiring clarification Possibility of future promotion Alternative possibilities within the organisation Possibilities for work elsewhere
Facts you can uncover needing further discovery Alternative options elsewhere Compromises you are willing to make for work Priorities of various elements in your life

Facts required from another
Availability of future promotion Possibilities within the organisation not yet public

Facts peripheral to the problem
Making a stand at work Avoiding confrontation Relationship with superior at work

It is invaluable to have taken the time here to think about facts of a conflict, and to access, realise and record them. This will create a good bank of information to begin the resolution exercise with. You may think that the facts of a conflict are obvious to you. However, skipping the thoughts provoked by this stage of the exercise and not starting with a full record of all possible relevant facts, is like beginning to build a house without a proper foundation.

Although things may seem okay and move quicker, the structure will crumble at a later stage and success in resolution may be jeopardised. The next stage in the process will be to start examining the feelings involved in the issues you are considering. I will look at this in the next chapter.

CHAPTER 6

Feelings

"Anger is an acid that can do more harm to a vessel in which it is stored than to anything on which it is poured"
Mark Twain

YOU NOW HAVE A note of your starting position on a conflict which you are considering, and a note of all the facts you think are relevant to the issues involved. As part of creating these notes, you will have noticed emotions surfacing. You may be aware of your usual emotional response when thinking of the conflict. The feelings you are experiencing now may be the same as this or they may be slightly different even at this early stage of the process. Below I will show you how to be aware of and manage your emotions.

Thought Patterns

You may have an accepted and ingrained emotional response to the issue you are considering. Often a cyclical pattern of reaction to a situation can arise. If a problem is left to fester and nothing is done to examine and address our response to it, the body and mind can just feel and think the same emotions and linked thoughts recurrently; each time the problem comes to mind the body and mind's set response is triggered. It could be that when you think of the problem area, you immediately feel, for example, angry. It is worth taking some quiet time to sit and try to plug into what other emotions arise over the conflict. It is also worth exploring to what the emotions you feel are linked; is it the conflict itself or something else? By accessing the real feelings evoked by the conflict, as a fresh exercise, the cycle of existing feelings and thoughts may be broken. We will look below at how this can effectively be achieved.

How to Access Your Full Range of Emotions

Breath is an important tool at your disposal. Breathing is often taken for granted; it has the power to break cycles of being carried along on a tide. Obviously, breath is needed to sustain life, however paying attention to the breath and slowing its pace can create calm in the body. Deliberately slower breath can reduce the hubbub of external influences on us, distil the thoughts and minimise the jumping around and racing back and forth in time of the mind, achieving concentration within our bodies at a given moment.

The power of long, deep, slow breathing has been recognised widely and is used in a variety of circumstances from Western childbirth to Eastern meditation. Within the Yogic tradition, breath can be used to stimulate the body by breathing quickly in and out through the nostrils (Breath of Fire) or conversely a long slow breath can be used to have a calming effect on the body. The joyous or victorious breath, (Ujjayi breath to give its Sanskrit term) is a breath which has been used during yoga practice for thousands of years, to achieve a slowing and calming effect on the body. The breath is slowly drawn in through the nostrils. The outbreath is restricted and slowed by restricting the epiglottis slightly. This can be achieved using the same action as that used to mist a mirror with your breath, but with the mouth closed. In fact, many of us will use a breath like this when feeling stressed, to let off steam and to relax ourselves. It is akin to a sigh; a natural and instinctive tool used by all of us to regain equilibrium.

Taking some time to still the mind and breathe slowly while being aware of a problem but not actively trying yet to resolve it can help us to understand how we deeply feel about it. You may find that underneath the anger is more deep-rooted feelings of sadness, desperation, hopelessness, frustration or hurt. It may well be those deeper feelings stem from your own personality and way of dealing with life or from the nature of your relationship with another. It can be very useful to uncover these buried emotions because solutions to the conflict may begin to be unearthed. It may also be that by recognising hitherto automated emotional responses, the conflict may begin to organically become less of an actual problem, as understanding emotions may hold a solution.

Try this exercise and see how you can access your emotions. Shut your eyes, take a few deep breaths, and focus calmly on how you feel. Use your breath to break the cycle of your established thoughts and emotions surrounding the conflict. Instead of going deeper into an established emotive pattern, find a way to feel your way through the conflict differently but with integrity. Telling yourself to not be angry is not an effective way of letting go of anger. Finding other sincere emotions within you to focus upon and explore instead of anger is practically useful in moving a conflict towards resolution. How did this make you feel? Maybe you began with a familiar feeling in relation to the conflict and then realised there were other feelings involved. Pay full attention to how you have felt carrying out this exercise. It is a good idea to record this so that you can notice all emotions and shifts in feelings. Below I look at the example conflicts and the emotions which could arise.

Example Conflicts and Emotions

Taking the first example of a conflict created about where to live, it could be that someone has frustration about living in a busy town. They feel they will be happier in the country, as that is where they spent their childhood. Yet maybe there is another element to the emotion; it could be that below the frustration there is a resentment of not being sufficiently heard in a relationship. Once the deeper emotion has been recognised, a possible solution begins to materialise in the form of working on communication with the other person. Maybe more autonomy or leadership in other areas of the relationship would result in feeling better about a joint decision as to where to live which appears to favour the other person's preferences.

Looking at the second example of an internal conflict created by serious injury, maybe the overwhelming feeling on the surface is one of hopelessness. The person may feel that they cannot control what has happened to them and they are thwarted in their life aims because of this unwanted circumstance. On further discovery of emotions, the person may feel that the hopelessness is connected to not being able to do a certain thing. It then becomes important to examine why there is a wish to do that particular thing. It may come from thought unconnected to real felt desires, or it may be a wish that was held at another time, no longer actually relevant. The possibility begins to open up that hopelessness could be resolved by reassessing the reality of the wish to achieve a certain thing. Maybe there are other deeply felt desires which could be formulated into new aims. Maybe these aims are achievable despite the injury.

In the case of the third example of a conflict at work, maybe there is an overriding feeling of unhappiness in a job. If a connection is made to deeper feelings, it may be that there is a frustrated need, say for mental stimulation and self-progression. Maybe concentrating on fulfilling those needs during work time, rather than the inadequacies of the job could possibly resolve the unhappiness.

Honesty with Feelings

Whatever the conflict, the real and best solution for you cannot be reached without knowing all the emotions which surround the issues involved. Fully realising those feelings may take more than a few minutes of quiet and deep breathing. However, once you are aware that deeper emotions may exist, you enter a phase where you allow yourself to recognise them.

You might begin to be more honest with yourself about the origins of your surface emotions. It may take some days or weeks of being aware of real emotions before you begin to realise how to address either those emotions or the conflict. There are practical tools for you to follow below, designed to assist the thought process and onward progression through a conflict to resolution. However, remember that small realisations (or even large ones), sometimes come when we are not thinking specifically about a problem. The fact that thoughts and feelings connected to the conflict have begun to be examined properly and freshly is enough to set the correct environment for progression towards resolution to begin to happen, not only during active concentration on the conflict. The reality of how you feel and why you feel that way may dawn in moments of doing something completely unconnected, or even during sleep. We are often told to 'sleep on it' when we have a decision to make, precisely to allow for this type of mind work. Having started the resolution process work, do not be afraid to leave space for answers to arise.

Once you have spent some time making space for the realisation of deeper feelings, it is fine to think about the subject and maybe analyse a bit about the way you feel. However, if this leads to entanglement and confusion remember to return to a quiet place of slower, deeper breathing, to reconnect with how you feel; not how you think you feel.

Try to record any feelings which arise, even if they don't appear to be connected to the conflict. You will be starting the process of accessing the full range of direct and indirect feelings you have concerning a particular conflict and its surrounding issues. This is very important work in understanding what you want from resolution and realising the emotional cost to you of continued conflict. You may not, before now, have been aware of the range and extent of your feelings here. Do not be concerned about feeling emotions and not knowing what to do about them. It may understandably, feel overwhelming to realise strong emotions. However, tapping into your feelings at this point, for the sake of awareness is all that is required. You will then be ready to begin the next phase of the resolution process, which involves a look back at the history of the conflict. Rather than dwelling on the past, I will next show you how to use the past instructively.

CHAPTER 7

History Pre-Conflict

"Insanity is doing the same thing over and over again and expecting different results"
Albert Einstein

ALTHOUGH IT IS IMPORTANT to be present in the current moment, giving your full attention to now, the past has importance and can show us much. The whole reason for the study of history is to look at past events, so that the good can be replicated and the bad can be avoided in the future.

Below I will encourage you to spend some time looking at any similar situations to this conflict you are looking at. It is good to look at how you or others you know have dealt with these situations either successfully, or unsuccessfully in the past. Look at approaches, attitudes or actions which might not have been your natural choice which have helped before, or which are your natural choice but have not helped in the past. There may be parallels with other past situations, which you or others have encountered, which have not occurred to you before now. Take instruction form the past, otherwise good things which have happened may be limited, and bad things have happened for nothing. Surveying the past also has another use. You may find, upon reflection, that the backdrop to the conflict holds clues for resolution.

How to Examine the Past

Take a moment to reflect on these questions: -

- What has been the history and build up to this conflict?
- Are there other unspoken or hidden issues which are a problem, behind the obvious ones?
- Have smaller issues been gathering unnoticed or has a current conflict been going on ignored for a while?

Maybe a current conflict is masking or diverting attention away from one or more other pertinent and possibly totally different problems. So other connected or seemingly unconnected past issues may exist, to which thought can be given to benefit the resolution of the current conflict directly or indirectly. Looking at some practical examples can help to clarify the sort of past events which can be relevant in a resolution process. This can start to allow you to make equivalent types of connections, even where circumstances, issues, background, or conflict have no direct parallel with an example.

Example Conflicts and Past History

Take firstly the first example of conflict over living location. It could be that this conflict is more about an imbalance of power generally between two people making a decision, than a problem with disagreement over where to live. Maybe there are areas of power imbalance which can be addressed, which might put the living location conflict into relief or shed light on the reasons for disagreement. It may be that looking at the history of the relationship and the way choices and joint decisions have been made in the past will be instructive as to how issues are being addressed now. This might reveal hidden problems and enable work to begin on a useful path towards corrections.

By allowing your thoughts to survey the past, you might find that problems you notice, once addressed could lead to possible natural resolution for this conflict. Alternatively, you might make corrections which when specifically applied to the current conflict, alter the dynamics of individual positions and hold a resolution solution. For one reason or another, the current conflict may effectively dissolve as a result of spotting and correction of past imbalances.

In the second example of conflict, of someone struggling with a life changing injury, maybe their life before was aimed at things which they could not realistically physically support. Maybe the things which are not attainable are being attached to the injury when they may just not be suited to the person. It could be that the life lived before the injury would be better for changes which now are being made due to the injury. There may be things which could be better for being different in the life of that person, regardless of the injury, but an inability to continue with certain things is being blamed on the injury and consequently life blockage is incorrectly or unfairly attributed to the injury. Resistance to change and a desire for life to be a certain way, emanating from the head rather than the heart, may be more at the centre of the conflict than the injury itself.

Turning to the third example of conflict, a problem at work, maybe there has been resentment to a senior at work for some time over issues other than the current one. Maybe there is an ingrained culture in the workplace which is more to blame for the problem than the specifics of the situation. There could have been mistakes, or perceived mistakes made in the past by an employee which have contributed to a course of action or attitude towards them which is not agreed with.

By looking at past issues with personalities, workplace culture and employee actions, thought and discussion can be allowed to begin. Where there is an objective problem identified in any of these areas, communication can take place to make corrections, or effort can be made to make positive actions which address or balance out past issues. Often making these changes or initiating discussion around them can organically lead to a resolution of the current conflict. If this does not directly happen, the path should start to clear towards future resolution. Often a study of the past will reveal that a current problem will only be perpetuated or repeated by not addressing past causes or contributing factors.

Patterns of the Past

Here a study of the past, of actions and reactions, can be a good way of noticing patterns, which might not be pinpointed without specific concentration on why a turn for the better or the worst may have happened. It is for this reason that people who struggle with certain conditions are encouraged to keep a diary of what they are doing and how they are feeling. Maybe you should start to record your own feelings and emotions over the conflict that you are experiencing. Looking back over such a record may bring into stark relief causes for certain mental or physical states which we would rather avoid if undesirable or encourage if helpful. It may be possible to identify some cycles, events or actions which lead to a repeated result, which had not been obvious to you from ordinary memory.

Often situations which arise in life leading to apparent conflict, can show us much if examined deeply. Conflict causes us to stop and think, to assess and re-assess things and to address issues. Without a conflict bringing things to a head, issues needing adjustment may continue unchecked. This could lead to further problems or conflicts of a worse nature. As such, conflict situations can be viewed as valuable opportunities to make positive adjustments to the way many things have been in the past. A conflict may represent and call attention to a long-standing problem simply waiting to be recognised and addressed. The benefits of looking at the conflict within the context of its specific past and the more general surrounding issues of the past could reach beyond the current conflict and well into the future.

Current Benefit

Retrospection is often not encouraged, as it can be seen as a waste of time to dwell on the past. Looking back can be seen as a practice which detracts from our giving the present our full attention. However, if we are looking at the past in a deliberate and thoughtful manner, with the intention of discovering new truths which can change our present and improve our future, this is surely to be encouraged. Links which exist between past problems, or between issues not even viewed formerly as problems, may be identified. Links between past issues and the current one which are not immediately obvious may be found. These links or themes are connections which would quite possibly not be made without looking back, within the conflict resolution exercise.

By surveying the past in a specific and general way there may be nothing identified which is thought to help with the current situation. If this is the case, a least there is confirmation and assurance in your mind. There is an elimination of the possibility of there being issues already existing which can help you now in the resolution process. If this is the case, it would be surprising, as most conflicts have background of some sort, even if not immediately obvious. In any case there is nothing to be lost in the process by including some thought surrounding the way the past has been. If in your judgment there is nothing instructive to be taken from past events or situations, you have the option of moving forward. However, try not to do this without full attention to this part of the exercise if clues as to resolution are not to be missed. It would surely be more of a waste of time and energy to undergo the exercise of attempting resolution without being thorough enough to achieve complete answers, than it would be to look back at the past. Be prepared to look back for a while and accept this as part of the eventual movement forward.

Having spent time examining the past, you may have found similarities and differences to other situations which you may wish to flag in your mind. Record these, so that you can use them to look at in future parts of the resolution exercise. This will remind you of what has worked or not worked with solving problems in the past. It will also be a record of things which have happened which may have led to or exacerbated the conflict. Do not worry about not being able to understand past situations fully as doing this work of surveying the past and recording relevant parts will mean that you can refer back to your thoughts and maybe continue to draw conclusions form the past, as the resolution exercise continues. Now you will be prepared to turn your attention to the future.

CHAPTER 8

The Future of the Conflict Area

"Our only true life is in the future"
George Orwell

LOOKING TO THE FUTURE is an important step in finding resolutions for conflicts. It is important to consider how you want the future to look generally and in relation to this conflict area. As mentioned in the previous chapter, we should always be mainly concerned with our present. However, what we decide in the present influences how our future takes shape and how we wish our future to be influences what we do in the present. Maybe a harmonious home or work life, or peace with yourself will be more important than the hitherto envisaged 'winning' solution to the current conflict. It could be that the harmony or peace which you desire can be strong enough to present you with a workable current solution, based on some change in your current views on the conflict subject, set off against benefits in other areas. The cost to our lives generally when bothersome conflict exists for us has always been recognised. How often have you heard someone saying, sometimes in desperation 'I would give anything to make this go away' or words to that effect? This is *why* it is good to look to the future. Below I will show you *how* to change perspective for a while to look to the future.

Considering Your Future

Take a moment to consider what you want your general future to look like.

Maybe the conflict is in an area which you can let go of and happily walk away from. If the area of your life has no place in your vision for the future, you can afford to find a solution for which a harmonious ongoing path connected to the conflict is not necessary to you. Sometimes this is the solution. If you do not need or want an ongoing personal or working relationship with a person and the disagreement is large enough to warrant the rift, you have more freedom with the solution. Conversely the problem may be to do with a relationship, situation or circumstance to which you are tied, or which you wish to be ongoing, especially if the conflict is internal.

So often in commercial mediations, an ongoing working relationship between waring companies, employees or business owners is so beneficial to both parties, that compromise on both sides over a conflict is truly worth it to salvage relations for the future path. Looking ahead to the future and what parties want from the future of the liaison can put the conflict into a different perspective. A mutually beneficial ongoing relationship is often to be seen in disagreements in the workplace, or more so with family members or spouses. It is clearly also the case that future harmony is paramount with internal conflicts as we are bound to ourselves in the future and any internal turmoil which can be settled is going to be worth settling to enhance the flow of our own future generally, in all areas of life.

Example Conflicts and Future Considerations

Returning to the examples will illustrate how considering the future can facilitate resolution. In the first example of a domestic conflict about where to live, it can be seen that the future is everything. A person in this position will need to gaze ahead at things they wish to do with their life and the way life may realistically be for them in the future. What are the really important things to that person to have in their life? Maybe they are yearning for a life in the country and the things that are important to them are their friends, exercise and hobbies. Will they still have access to their friends as easily after a move? Will it be easy to exercise in bad weather with no gyms nearby? Will there be local groups for the interests of the person?

By looking closely at the detail desired from future life, there might come a realisation that in certain circumstances ease of obtaining or getting to work, for example, might be more important than ability to exercise and participate in hobbies. Maybe the envisaged country life is idealised or not totally in line with the reality of the way of life for that person will be. If current working needs to continue, maybe that happening easily is more important to a relaxed life than pastimes. Examining the future by looking at the way that person desires life to be and how life is likely to be in each location can highlight any discrepancy between the conflict position and the future of the person.

It seems obvious to point out that arguing a position in a conflict should be what a person really wants. However, until the future is properly examined, what that person truly wants for the future might not actually come to light. Sometimes a position arises because it is historic and no longer actually relevant. If there are no deeper problems surrounding the conflict, this sort of disagreement can dissolve when the future is examined in detail. Other times a position can be held to make a stand or 'win' a point. In that case there could be issues around power imbalance or perceived imbalance to address. It is possible that one person is just being stubborn without full reason and may drop that after discussion. Whatever the situation, a good hard look at the future of the conflict area and future life wellbeing all round will help to see the conflict in perspective and to highlight issues which will really be beneficial to that person's life to address.

In the second conflict example, if someone has a problem with a serious injury, which they feel is stopping them from for example from going on a dream holiday, there are many questions about the future to ask.
- What is important to that person's future and is the holiday central to that?

- Is the need to be satisfied by the holiday likely to be capable of being met in a different way?

Maybe a shorter, closer or different type of holiday could provide the benefit sought while bringing additional benefits of ease in many areas. It could be that embarking on a totally different venture could provide the change and interest sought if it is a new and different adventure which is behind the strong desire. What will life with the holiday look like and is it desirable and sustainable? It could be that any benefits of rest on the holiday will be cancelled out by the journey back, the cost and the pile of things not addressed while away.

Starting to look at the future in this way reduces the conflict to a cost or risk/benefit analysis, not particular to someone with an injury, whilst maybe having different elements to consider. Realisations such as this can begin to resolve the feeling of conflict itself. What it will be like organising and paying for the holiday; whether it is a desirable thing both to work towards and in the long term are all relevant future considerations. Is the holiday period itself the only real benefit? What are the true benefits to future life of having the holiday and are there any benefits of not going on this specific holiday? Although it sounds odd when we are lamenting the lost opportunity to do something we would have planned or liked to do, it is interesting to look at how the mechanics of the course of action would affect future life. Often there will be a cost to investing time, effort and resources in a particular thing and so conversely there will be a saving in not doing it.

By truly looking at the future in an inquisitive way both with and without this dream travel, can be enlightening as to the conflict and how to resolve it. As with disagreements with another, internal conflict can often be about clinging stubbornly to deep-rooted ideas or thoughts. Sometimes it can be about wanting something we feel we cannot have maybe just precisely because we feel we cannot have it. Looking ahead to the future having the thing we are chasing (in this case a dream holiday) and how life will really be with and without that can sometimes show us that the thing we have conflict over is not something which will truly change our life at all, let alone for the better, either uniquely or at all.

Alternatively looking to the future may convince a person of the absolute benefit of the holiday, in terms of arranging it, experiencing it and how life will be afterwards, in which case resolution may lie in finding a way to achieve this holiday or a similar acceptable alternative one, despite the injury.

In the third example of conflict in a workplace problem where an employee has maybe been denied promotion, the envisaged resolution for that employee up until now may have been for a demand for current recognition and immediate promotion. However, if the employee begins to imagine the future and how they would wish things to be, they might realise that their current promotion might create an atmosphere difficult to work in. Maybe superiors would not trust the work of the employee in an elevated role at this stage or perhaps peers would resent the promotion, or subordinates lose respect due to events.

Given that promotion has been denied these questions needs to be asked:

- Would the reasons behind this disintegrate with a reversal of the decision?
- Would further unrest be created by changing a decision already put in place, which might be difficult to work within?

It could be that this employee would benefit from a period of consolidating their work reputation and proving themselves as able to carry out the higher role. By not making immediate demands and establishing a continued and solid proof of ability, the employee may arrive at a point for promotion in the future, where there is trust, goodwill and respect surrounding them from superiors, peers and subordinates. It could be that this atmosphere is worth waiting for and that the future created by delaying a promotion request can be seen as more desirable than an immediate promotion with little prospects of harmony surrounding the role. Looking to the future in this way may allow the conflict situation to give rise to altered efforts which lead to an improvement in the actual work of the employee, or in the way that they formally request and receive recognition for their work. Of course, the expectation of future change can be managed in a suitable way; perhaps by stating in advance that an effort is being made to prove ability, or by drawing attention to the efforts after they are under way.

It could be that by looking to the future, the employee realises that a role within the current workplace is not actually what their heart desires. Perhaps they realise that the desired role is not going to come their way or that they cannot imagine themselves happily in the role in question or do not actually want to do the job involved in the promotion.

Whatever conflict we are in, sometimes we become so caught up in the apparent current injustice to us of a situation, that we can lose sight of what we want or what is best for us going forward. It could be that this workplace conflict situation becomes the catalyst for change to another role or workplace which is a better fit.

Paving the way for a workable and harmonious future does not mean accepting anything at any cost now. It does not mean automatically dropping your preferences, needs, aspirations and dreams. Of course, boundaries must be established and set with others and for oneself. Looking at the value of the conflict area or relationship to you in the future will help in the setting of these boundaries.

Ask These Questions:

- What is the area of conflict you are facing?
- How do you think that area of your life looks in the future?
- How do you wish the future to look?
- What are your short, medium, and longer-term general aspirations in life?
- How does the conflict area fit in with this?

Setting Boundaries

Putting thought into the value to you of a conflict area in terms of harmony with others or yourself and how important that is to you is often work which leads to some evaluation of a conflict, in terms of where boundaries should be set. In fact, the boundaries themselves are crucial and often the requests or absolutes, as well as the concessions involved in the settlement of conflicts, will serve to strengthen a future relationship or area of life. Being tough or realistic with another or oneself is valuable work for the future. Establishing logical or heartfelt base line expectations from the outcome of the conflict is crucial to its resolution. This is likely to happen when the future itself of the conflict area and the value of it to you is given full consideration as part of the conflict management process. It is tempting to view any free thought about the future as an exercise in justifying an inevitable capitulation. However, the exercise is all about benefit to you both within the conflict and in wider life. Keeping this in mind will keep your expectations and any requests realistic and balanced, because they will be seen in the setting of the total real value of the outcome to you.

A survey of the future and what it looks like for you in this conflict area and generally, is a vital step in beginning to realise the real worth to your life of resolving the conflict. It is also a start to establishing perspective in the conflict area as compared to your life in general. The next step in evaluation and perspective is to realistically examine the strengths and weaknesses of your position on a conflict, which is the next topic we will look at.

CHAPTER 9

Strengths and Weaknesses

"Men are apt to mistake the strength of their feeling for the strength of their argument. The heated mind resents the chill touch and relentless scrutiny of logic"
William E. Gladstone

WHATEVER THE STRENGTHS OF your position on a conflict matter, there will be weaknesses. There will be other points which you perceive as strengths which are only so from your point of view. It is natural to see things from your own viewpoint primarily and to favour your own position. If you did not do this there would be no disagreement, problem or conflict in the first place. Below I will show you how to start to be more objective about this. The viewpoint you are aiming for is still very much your own. However, it will be from the position of having applied reality to some points you may just be accepting currently.

Often a standpoint, way of viewing things or the position you see as correct has arisen without much direct thought. Up until the decision to work on a conflict, your position on it will usually have arisen from simply acting, thinking, and feeling as you chose to do. We usually chose to do and think the things which we think are right. Sometimes we try to make the things we think and do right by justifying them, because we generally like to think we are right in our thoughts and actions.

When circumstance brings the conflict to us, we tend to think it is unfair and when a person brings the conflict, we tend to think they are wrong. Any possible wrong on our part we tend to justify, gloss over or dismiss as irrelevant, as natural human nature. Although we may accept fault in other circumstances, any substantial blame on our own part for a problematic conflict is unlikely to have been accepted, because this would more than likely have averted any crisis point. People can find themselves at a point where problematic conflict arises after a period of bobbing along, maybe with small niggles, or alternatively realising a rising wave of discord. It can seem that the conflict has been laid at our feet for no good reason.

Strengths

It is important to look at the things we see as strengths or our correct actions, thoughts, and feelings in relation to the conflict area. Looking at weaknesses is a more obvious area for examination and that is covered below.

- Is it possible that things you have accepted as right are things which have slipped a bit?

- Is it perhaps the case that you have allowed yourself to justify things which have strayed from the black and white of what you accept?

It is sometimes the case that we construct a universe around us which runs to our rules, in our mind. This can happen when we continue on a path of thinking, unchallenged and in a bubble. This is why people discuss important life matters and decisions with family, close friends and people they trust and respect, to get a second opinion. How often after asking someone else's opinion, have you had cause to pause for thought, or maybe become irritated by a different viewpoint or less than enthusiastic backing?

Often on close examination things which we are sure about can start to fall into a grey area. The first step in applying objectivity and an honest overview to a conflict area is to re-trace events or actions and to look afresh at how they have arisen. Start to question all things, but specifically those you have viewed as right as well as those you have accepted as wrong, which have fuelled the conflict. Look specifically at the matters you have seen up until now to strongly support your position and examine them.

Many a time in my former professional work as a Barrister I would receive written accounts or speak in conference to a person in dispute with another and be presented with arguments or issues within or considered to support their main case, which they had long been totally convinced as watertight points in their favour. Some of these were not matters which held; they were either legally or objectively unrealistically in their favour. We all do this. It is natural to try to convince ourselves and others of our own validity and integrity. Once we believe we are right overall about a situation, the minor details of possible error can fall by the way and become lost in the grand scheme of being right.

Weaknesses

It is a good exercise, of course, to examine what you accept as weaknesses to your position in detail, rather than dismiss them as minor or difficult to think about. In an argument or legal battle, what you consider to be a small weakness could scale up into something which makes the whole thing go against you. Points in favour of the other side which you might not agree with or wish to accept could objectively weaken your own standpoint. You may already be aware of some of these weaker points, which are not in your favour in the conflict, but you might be ignoring or not focusing upon them. It is a good idea as part of this exercise to allow yourself to focus on matters which you consider as weaknesses. You can ponder why they are weaknesses and how far they are strengths for the other person or situation against you.

Example Conflict Strengths and Weaknesses

The theoretical and real strengths and weaknesses of a situation can be illustrated by the usual examples here again. In the first example of conflict, if there is a domestic conflict about living location, the party advocating town living may consider a strength of their argument to be proximity to amenities. When examined more closely this strength may become questionable if a rural location is found which is well served by facilities itself. On a closer look it might become clear that the rural location not only has good amenities but has a stronger local community attached to facilities, offering help and support to residents. In this scenario you can see that what was considered a strong argument for town living, could become a comparative weakness, to be re-considered.

The same person within the couple conflict of where to live, who prefers the town as a location may always have accepted that the lower level of clean air and tranquillity was an accepted weakness in their argument. Here it can be seen that clearly, they should take a close look at how light, noise and chemical pollution will affect the couple, their health and their plans for the future. Rather than shrugging this off as an obvious point, but irrelevant perhaps because they prefer the hustle and bustle of city life, the element of this consideration and how it affects life should be examined. This shows that an obvious point of weakness needs thorough consideration.

In the first example of conflict, a disagreement over where to live, both persons' feelings may be important to acknowledge, but practicalities may take a higher priority in the decision of location. For example, the location may support a job or jobs without which the family could not sustain itself. That is not to say that feelings are not a strong factor in the conflict, or cannot be met in some other way, but the priority of important practicalities may mean that the argument to answer to feelings alone may be weakened. On the other hand, if the feelings connected to a preference for location are so strong that they are affecting the wellbeing of a person, there could be a case for this argument being stronger than the practical one, which on the face of it may take priority. Here it can be seen that accepted strengths and weaknesses of a position may be given varying weights of importance, and their ranking could change when considered alongside other factors.

Now take the second example of conflict, the case of a serious injury, which seems to the injured person to be a reason why their life has been negatively affected. With internal conflicts, like the struggle over an unwanted injury or a bad situation, a strong disadvantage can be likened to the 'strength' of a more usual argument type conflict. The injured person might see the biggest disadvantage of their situation being that their partner is very active and they can no longer engage in activities together. The so-far accepted disadvantage of the injury might be the view that it leads to many arguments between the couple. This point, viewed as a strong disadvantage of the injury, causing relationship problems should be looked at fully.

Consider this:

- Are activities of the sort enjoyed by the other partner still possible for the injured person?

- If yes, are they desirable for that person?

- If no, is the other partner content to pursue those activities outside the relationship?

On deeper examination it could become more possible that the reason for not engaging in the activities together is preference rather than physical ability, therefore, not to be blamed upon the injury. It might alternatively become clear that the other partner has decided to question the relationship for reasons totally separate from the lack of engaging in activities or results of the injury. Maybe the person with injury has an insecurity about being seen not to be able to do things, where the other partner really does not mind. Maybe the injured person has a fear about trying to engage in activities and failing to be able to, or a fear of making the injury worse through activity (founded or unfounded), or even pure frustration about limitations caused by the injury.

The real disadvantage here is the conflict the injured person feels within themselves in having the injury and its effect on their life, rather than problems between the couple caused by the injury itself. Arguments may have pre-existed between the couple. Maybe obvious alternative main reasons for differences have been glossed over, with the injured person convinced that but for the injury the relationship would be fine. Proper delving into the nature, cause and frequency of arguments may show a deeper problem all together. Maybe the arguments are nothing to do with the injury.

Here what was viewed as a strong disadvantage of the injury becomes irrelevant to the way life has gone.

The premise that the injury has ruined the relationship becomes a fallacy and the central real reason for the turn which life has taken becomes non-compatibility with the other person, or frustration of the injured person. The injury may now be seen as a less problematic area in so far as the effect upon the relationship. It may be that the injury was an original reason for abstinence from a couple of activities on an occasional basis or a catalyst for some initial arguments. It might not necessarily follow that abstinence from activities is either the cause of the friction or the fault of the injury and the arguments may generally be present regardless of injury or be just blamed on the injury from habit. Again, what seemed like a strong disadvantage of the injury situation becomes a weaker point on examination. There are clues here that the root of conflict could be the injured person's attitude to the injury and not the injury itself.

The injured person's will to live their life in a way in which they could if well seems a strong disadvantage in an injury conflict. However, the possibility of other less physical and more practical achievements and the need to be kind to one's own body are overriding factors which weaken the strength of the original disadvantage. Maybe living life as before the injury led to the injury situation. Focusing on the importance of arguments against what you wish for is sometimes helpful to gain good perspective on your desires and frustrations.

In the third example of conflict over a job, there could be a workplace conflict where a particular task, seen as a promotion has been assigned to another employee, leaving someone in conflict over not having the challenge or kudos of attending to the task themselves. In this case, the individual with the conflict problem may consider a strength of their argument for being assigned the task, to be their ability to perform well. A weakness may be that they have not been employed as long as the person to whom the task has actually been assigned. The employee may realise both these points and have them at the back of their mind.

The points may even start to link up; the strength of belief in ability to perform a task may make the weakness of less time in the job appear irrelevant. However, how strong is the stronger argument? Is the belief in ability based on experience or proven ability or is it linked solely to a strong will and desire to be assigned the task? It may be possible that a superior deciding about assignment of the task has been required to take evidence of past ability as a main indicator of suitability for the task. This could be a formal part of a fair selection process for assigning tasks. What was a strong point of this conflict thus becomes weaker on closer examination.

The acknowledged weaker point of having spent less time in the job may now become quite pertinent and not just an irrelevant side issue. Giving due consideration to the weakness of less experience is now important. Maybe there has not been enough time for the employee to prove themselves as able to take on a particular task. The linked stronger and weaker issue now join to form a logical argument against assignment of the task, rather than arguments joining together to back up a case for being given the task. Through proper examination of what were viewed as both stronger and weaker points in the position on this conflict, a viewpoint may start to change. A way to manage the conflict may start to emerge as the employee realises that time needs to be spent working and proving themselves within their job and gathering evidence of ability. It might be possible to start resolution by bringing attention to the fact that the next six months will be spent achieving this experience and proving ability, with relevant opportunities being agreed to be provided and results agreed to be recorded. This might facilitate consideration for assignment of a similar task to that sought in a few months' time.

In the case of an impediment in the work environment causing conflict, it may be that even if a person fervently desired a promotion and was good enough to deserve it, a strong opposing argument might be that the person who ultimately was given the desired position was in fact better equipped to carry out the role. Recognising such a fact can help one to accept that although an outcome was not the desired one, the decision was based on an understandable logic. Maybe the argument 'I've been here longer, and I deserve the extra salary', would seem strong, it soon weakens in the light of the promoted person being better qualified and actually more able to focus on the specific job. Here again, a weaker point in the conflict of losing a promotion may be another's ability, which should be given due consideration, to gain proper perspective.

Risk

A further matter to be taken into consideration along with weaknesses of your position is the inherent risk that things will not go your way if you do not take control of resolution. Even where a conflict is dealt with in the formal way through the court system, it is always the case when a non-criminal matter goes to court that even a strong case can fail. Partly this is due to the civil standard of proof which is just 'on the balance of probabilities' and not beyond reasonable doubt. The outcome of the application of the civil standard by judges often sitting alone in small matters in the County Courts and larger matters in the High Courts in England and Wales, is that individual judgments can vary.

A case is also only judged on the evidence brought before the court on the day. So even in a matter which goes all the way to court for a decision, things may not go the way you expect them to. There may be matters not brought before the court, unexamined history or emotions not taken into account. This shows how much general risk there can be over the outcome from a formal settling of a dispute and even professional opinions and ensuing outcomes can vary. What this illustrates is that there are other valid points of view and a strong point, even when professionally argued, can be weak if viewed in a different way or not backed by the same evidence. Conversely a weak point can be given more weight than it has been previously assigned, if fully considered and argued well. The variance in professional opinions and outcomes, based on the same facts shows how matters can be seen very differently on examination.

The advantage of settling a matter privately through conflict resolution is that you are in control of the issues raised, discussed, considered, and dismissed. You are not limited as to what comes into the mix in reaching a conclusion. Neither are you dependant on another person nor a set of rules governing the result of your disagreement; any solution is possible. However, being objective and realistic is vital if you are to successfully resolve a conflict.

Realism

Therefore, it can be seen that examining how strong the considered strengths of your position on a conflict are and looking objectively at the weaknesses of your position can bring important realisations. Being realistic and practical about a conflict is a necessary step which follows and is part of this exercise. Once you have loosened the tie between you and your position, its justification and total blind support for it, you will begin to be able to explore further areas, which could hold acceptable solutions for you. It is also the case that when you begin to let go of the grip on your position the sometimes fierce emotions surrounding that also begin to dissipate allowing for a wider view point.

Once you have taken a fresh and realistic view of the strengths and weaknesses of your position on a conflict area, you will be starting to gain objectivity. As with previous stages, it is good to record the strengths and weaknesses you have considered and the thoughts which have come up about them. It can feel quite disarming to be accepting new evaluation, but do not worry about this. No conclusions are needed yet and the shifts which happen during the whole resolution process are gradual. You will have completed the groundwork to move on to the next stage of resolution, examined below, which involves looking at your own needs and interests.

CHAPTER 10

Needs and Interests

"An eye for an eye will only make the whole world blind"
Mahatma Gandhi

ONCE YOU HAVE THOUGHT about your position on the dispute (and anyone else's position, who is relevant to the conflict) and the realistic strengths and weaknesses of that, you will be able to start to focus upon what you want to achieve from the conflict resolution process. You should focus now on your needs and interests. The movement from concentrating on your position on the conflict to beginning to focus on your specific and general needs and interests is crucial to the resolution process. Below I will show you how to start to make the shift, which professional mediators strive to achieve. It is the movement from what you want as an outcome based on anger and revenge towards an acceptance of a peaceful solution which you need, in order to live well and move forward in your best interest.

Life Goals

Whether you have a disagreement with another or a situational conflict, take time to think about your personal goals in life. To begin with, your goals and aims may seem unconnected to the problem in question. However, conflicts will almost certainly disrupt personal goals and aims. There may be disruption in terms of a toxic relationship, conflict blocking harmonious progress or reputational issues. It is certainly the case that the cost in terms of time and stress of a problem (in additional to any financial costs) will interrupt achievement in other areas.

For example, imagine you have a developing dispute with a neighbour, and your personal goal is simply to live a happy life. The conflict and tension created by a dispute of which you will be reminded on a daily basis through contact with your neighbour will affect your wellbeing. You will have less acrimonious and happier things upon which to spend your precious time and money. The stress of a dispute and maybe even of possible court proceedings will affect your ability to relax and concentrate on the nicer things in life. The stress of the dispute, pressures of time involved, and financial risk may well affect close relationships and thereby add to your unhappiness. Settling the dispute will certainly lead to finality in terms of financial risk, time spent on the issue and stress generated by a continued dispute. If relationship issues are improved by the conflict management process, there may be further benefits in harmonious living. You may be willing to compromise to a certain extent on your best outcome to benefit from the closure brought about by the resolution of the dispute.

Alternatively, think about your company, or a company you work for being in dispute with a customer. The aim of the company is to generate profit and maybe also to grow. The dispute will be taking up company resources in terms of time and money. It will be diverting these resources away from profit-making work. The dispute may also risk damaging the reputation of the company, which could affect existing customers or possible future ones, therefore hampering growth. Business with the customer in question may be suspended due to the dispute. Again, it is clear to see that the dispute is affecting the aims of the company. It may be more profitable for the company to compromise financially over this dispute in the conflict management process and reap the rewards of time and resources freed up to generate profits elsewhere. If relations with the customer to whom the dispute relates are improved enough, further business may be resumed in that area.

Needs

Generally, we all have basic psychological and physical needs; once these are met our needs move towards improving our situation and ourselves. The psychologist Maslow's model of the 'hierarchy of needs', developed in 1943, pointed out the pyramid nature of our needs as humans, starting with basic needs at the bottom of the pyramid and culminating in our aspirations at the top. However, because most people in the Western world have their basic needs met, they tend to concentrate on aspirations and these become more important, in effect inverting the pyramid. When looking at your needs and interests, think not only about those things that you need to survive, but also those things you want in order to thrive. These are your aims, in more general terms than the settling of the conflict.

Your Aims

Consider how much it is really worth to you to settle your conflict. What price would you put on being able to continue with a happy stress-free life or to progress in your job? We will return later to the focus on a happy life with any overall aims clearly possible to be achieved and the feeling that creates. It may facilitate the summarising of your aims if you consider the categories in the following diagram. This is provided as an overview and there will be an opportunity for the detailed recording of your aims later.

Categories of Personal Aims

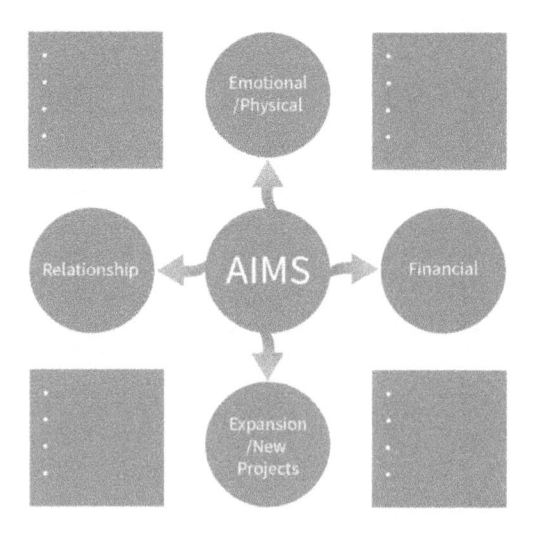

Aims of Each Party

You may wish to consider not only your interests and needs in this exercise but also perhaps those of anyone else involved in this conflict, which are known to you. Of course, you will be guessing about this, but you may be in a good position to make an educated guess at their needs and interests. You may know whether they are the same as yours or different. If your conflict is internal or situational, you can think in terms of the results of a situation.

Aims Diagram

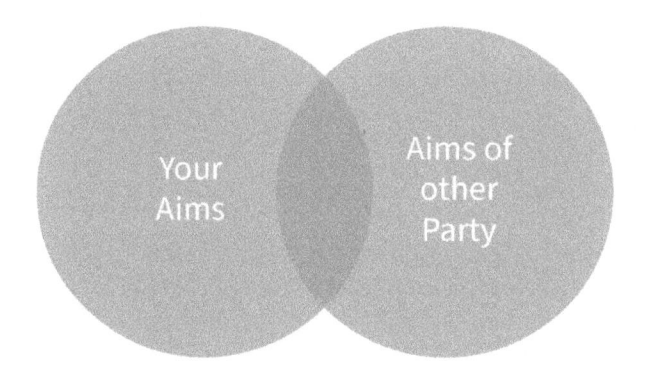

It is important to think about the areas shown in this figure:

a) your aims;
b) the other party's aims; and
c) any joint aims.

You will see that the above figure shows an area of intersection between the aims of the two parties to a dispute. I am showing you this now so that you will understand where you are headed. Start to think about where your aims and the aims of the other party may coincide. Common areas of aims may be ground for negotiation or exploration during the conflict management process.

You will save valuable time and gain efficiency and effectiveness in the process if you can begin to address all three depicted aim areas, in whatever way you can. This may seem like much to think about but there is no need to become too concerned with the answers to the intersection of aims now. The stages of thinking about and recording your aims and those of another will be covered below. Ideas alone are useful at this stage; there is no need to reach definite conclusions, as the process is aimed at developing these. The more thoughts and broad thinking you can start to achieve, the more successful the process is likely to be as an exercise taking your disagreement towards an acceptable resolution.

I will return to the example conflicts below in more detail to illustrate aims of another and where they might overlap with your own. With internal conflict or situational conflict, think in terms of the results of the situation, rather than aims of another. In effect the intersection of your aims and the results of a conflict situation, will be the advantages of the situation. Maybe you have only considered the negatives up until now?

The theory of 'goal congruence' was put forward by R. G. May, G. H. Mueller and T. H. Williams, in the mid 1970's. It was a management accounting tool which advocated the development by a company of its employees' personal aims. By doing this, the theory supported corporate advancement by reason of the aims of the company being aligned with the aims of the employees; both company and employees would benefit from mutual advancement of aims through the company. This theory has had supporters and dissenters over the years, but points towards the importance of matching aims to promote mutual harmony and advancement, and as such is worth noting.

If the conflict is an internal problem or a situation with which you are struggling, your aims are the same with or without the conflict. It is important to take time to clarify your life aims. It may be that these aims are changed from what they may have been in the past, because of the situation you are in. If that is the case, there is even more reason to solidify your current aims and to focus on them. Use the space below to record aims which you have in any area you can think of. I have included some examples to help start your thought process. There will be an opportunity to return to the subject of life aims in more detail, in Chapter 13 so there is no need to feel undue pressure now with your ideas. The notes added are only intended as limited examples, which may or may not be relevant, and can certainly be added to.

Your Aims	Notes
Personal Development	New Skills
Physical Improvement	Concentration on Diet and Exercise

Mental Improvement	Meditation/Time alone
Family Situation	Children/Grandchildren/Caring for Parents
Career Development	Change of Job/Promotion
Lifestyle Changes	More Time Abroad/Holidays
Achievements	Working on a Project

The above exercise can be repeated to try to access the aims of another person involved in a conflict, or the results of a situation. The lists can then be compared to find any overlaps.

Example Conflicts and Aims

To return to the examples which have been followed throughout, take the first example of conflict, the conflict created by a difference in opinion over where to live. The aim of one person may be to feel freer and more at one with nature by living in the countryside. Meanwhile the other person may prefer the ease of access to work and the company of living in a more populated and serviced urban setting. On examination of the aims of both parties, it can become clear that each wants to live a stress-free life. While the ideas of each on what constitutes stress may vary, the aim is something in common. For one person the practicality of convenience and less commuting creates a desirable freedom; for the other the feeling of space and nature creates a similarly desirable freedom. It may be possible to find a location where there is convenience combined with the rural feel. That may be a house on the outskirts of town with a large garden, or adjacent to parkland. It may be a house in the country with facilities to work from home, or near a work hub where a potential job could be arranged. Shifting from a stubborn and ingrained position on preference to looking at the reasons for the preference in conjunction with life aims can produce possible solutions.

Looking at the second example of conflict over the development of an unwanted serious injury, maybe the feeling of frustration comes from not being able to do things which used to be possible, or which could be possible without certain physical or mental limitations. If the person with an injury looks at their life aims, maybe they will realise that they are ambitious or competitive by nature and need progress for fulfilment. Maybe that progress could make use of what they have learned from the injury. If the limitations brought by the injury are physical, maybe the progress could be mental, or in the form of slower but still sure progress towards an aim. If the limitations are mental, maybe the progress could involve more action than thought. There are always some things that can be achieved, no matter what the restrictions on a person. Adaptation can work but only if the final aim is something thought to be worthwhile. It is important to be creative, just because a person always wanted to do something, and maybe more so now that they feel that they cannot, doesn't mean they cannot achieve the same end feeling by choosing something else to accomplish.

Turning to the third example a conflict over dissatisfaction at work, the employee may find that they are fixed on a certain promotion which has been denied. What is it of importance that the person will gain from the promotion? Is it higher financial reward, or the kudos of an elevated position or maybe just the recognition of service? Depending on the specific importance behind the denied promotion, perhaps that same aim can be achieved by that person in a different way (for example, by applying for a different position within the organisation, or even a job elsewhere). Or maybe once the specific aim and reason for the aim has been identified, it can be discussed further at work and maybe achieved in the same workplace in a different way (for example, by a pay rise within the same role, a re-naming of a position, or a special recognition other than promotion).

The work you have completed here will tie in with the exercise of looking at the future. Whatever the conflict, looking past it towards the way that you would wish the future to be in life, can help to put the specifics of the conflict into perspective. By then focusing on your aspirations and aims for the future, the intense focus is diverted away from the conflict and towards the general forward flow of your life. This in turn helps to show ways in which the conflict can perhaps be dealt with to your overall benefit, even if not in the specific way you had originally envisaged.

Here the feeling of beginning to see the conflict as less important, in comparison to life needs and interests, may be uncomfortable, especially if you have spent a period of time attached to your position on the problem. Do not be concerned about this, you are reaching what is often a turning point in resolution. This can happen without full awareness of a change in view, but as a result of surrounding thoughts being developed. Sometimes battles are lost but wars are won. What you might have viewed as a defeat could be somehow in your favour. You have seen how to keep your eye on the end prize and the things you value as important from life. It is vital to keep moving towards that point and not to become stuck or frozen by distractions along the way. Keep your focus as you now move towards broader thinking.

CHAPTER 11

Broader Thinking

"There are three truths: my truth, your truth and the truth"
Chinese Proverb

THERE ARE VARIOUS TECHNIQUES which a skilled mediator will employ to encourage parties to think more broadly about their situation. It can be useful to employ some of these in your own conflict resolution exercise and I will show you the techniques below. This will not detract from a successful outcome for you, and it should be stressed that is not suggested in order to bring about wholesale capitulation. The advantage of thinking more broadly is that it may enable you to bring more ideas to the conflict management process, or even just encourage a less fixed and narrow way of thinking, opening the door to the possibility of resolutions not envisaged. Great thinkers have often noted the advantages of thinking in a different way. Einstein said, "We cannot solve our problems with the same thinking we used when we created them." It may feel somewhat derailing, but do not be put off by this; as Tolstoy wrote "Once we are thrown off our habitual paths, we think all is lost, but it's only here that the new and the good begins."

Brainstorming

One useful technique is 'brainstorming'. This technique involves the generating of as many solutions to the problem as can be thought of. It is important not to dismiss any ideas which occur, or to try to evaluate the effectiveness or practicality of any idea when it first occurs. All ideas which come to mind should be written down initially. The ideas can then be worked through one by one, giving each idea enough consideration to assess whether there is any merit to it, maybe in conjunction with employing a difference in approach.

Embarking upon this exercise in a quiet, private manner can have the advantage of thought free from time pressure or inhibition of the proximity of any other party. It may even be that a thought generated at this stage and dismissed upon further consideration, may be recalled and revisited later when shifts could make the idea more feasible as a solution. Use the diagram below to start to record as many possible solutions as occur to you. Record every idea, aiming for quantity rather than quality, without any initial judgment. Add branches to the diagram as required and the same diagram can be used again for the generation of solutions to other issues within the main dispute.

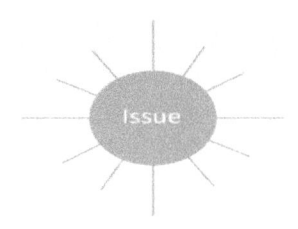

Dispute Issues and Brainstormed Solutions

An extension of the brainstorming technique is the fishbone diagram. This involves taking an issue and examining the component parts to it, identifying causes and effect. This can be used to prioritise issues within a disagreement or situation.

Cause and Effect Fishbone Diagram

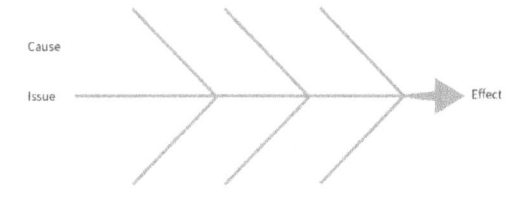

Part of thinking more broadly is to look at what the past can show you, as covered earlier. Remember to consider if there are any things which you wouldn't usually do, which you have done in the past and have helped situations then, so might work here. Are there things you have done in the past which have made things worse and so should be avoided? As mentioned above, the past might hold clues, not immediately obvious to you, which could lead to resolution solutions.

Again, as covered above your future aspirations for life and the part the conflict area can play within that, or to clear the way for that should be considered. Although thinking in the present is a good practice, it should not blinker you either from the past as instruction or from the broader road ahead of you.

As referred to earlier, when considering facts, try to consider unknown matters of relevance to the conflict as part of wider thought on the topic, in line with Rumsfeld's thinking. Remember that unknown matters may be both known at some level or totally unknown to you. Include the possibility of researching or uncovering areas connected to the conflict.

Something Blocking Resolution

Try to think more widely about whether there is anything holding you back from resolving your conflict.

- Do the conflict issues mask another problem or divert you from areas you do not wish to think about?

- Is the conflict reinforced by an established pattern of thoughts or behaviour rather than a true conflict?

- Could a different attitude to a situation ease the conflict?

- Have you been stalling on trying to resolve the issues for some reason?

Ask yourself these questions and be honest and allow yourself to consider these possibilities.

All of the above will create the right frame of mind for broad, objective, and creative thinking. Once freed from the narrow path of your habitual thought around the conflict area to date, possible solutions will start to open up. All the groundwork to arrive at this point is an important part of the resolution process. Once broader thinking has been established you will be able to concentrate on the specifics of the reality of how a conflict situation is and how you wish things to be in the future. It should then start to become possible to relate the present to your future to achieve progression from one to the other. You will now have moved away from your original positional view sufficiently to start to see how the conflict can be shaped into a situation which can yield to and support your chosen direction for the future.

Try to keep this broader perspective in mind in the next sections, where thinking becomes narrower again for a while, in order to reinforce specifics which, make up the big picture of your life. When you begin to look at specifics of a conflict area now and in the future, it can be easy to be drawn back into original patterns of circular thought, which may have fuelled the conflict up until now. Watch out for any slipping back and negative thoughts which return you to a point of deadlock and despair for solution to the conflict. If this begins to happen it is good to take a break and to attempt to go back to the wider thought which has been established now.

Wide thought is consistent with a feeling that things will work out if certain important basics are maintained, established, and aimed for. When we start to look at specifics, we can become bogged down by the detail. Hold the feeling of wider thought and many possibilities for solution and movement forward, as you tackle the detail of realistic strands pulled from this exercise and how they look. This will stop you from slipping back to a feeling of being defeated by the conflict situation.

Remember the feeling of hope and wide possibility established at this stage of the exercise, for example by brainstorming. If necessary, you can return to this part of the resolution exercise at any time you feel overwhelmed by the gap in detail of getting from where you are on a conflict to where you want to be. It can be important to remember this because the movement away from a firmly held position, backed by a reinforced thought pattern, can be a disarming process which creates a feeling of vulnerability. Not being anchored to a set requirement and accepted 'right' outcome from a conflict situation can create doubt about the conflict and your own thinking and ability to successfully resolve it. This is a normal part of the process and should not be allowed to knock you off course. The next stage will involve looking at the realistic situations for you without a resolution in this conflict.

CHAPTER 12

Best and Worst Alternatives to a Resolution

"When you go to war as a boy, you have a great illusion of immortality"
Ernest Hemmingway

IN THE WORLD OF mediation, encouraging parties to think about the best and worst outcomes without an agreed resolution acts as an important reality test. Now you are encouraged to do the same, in your own way, for your own problem being considered.

Best Outcome

The best outcome without a resolution will be everything you want, all the recompense you seek, with no blame or costs of any sort apportioned or falling to you. Although this would be an ideal scenario with no risk to you, thinking about the probability of everything going your way, perhaps after a failed attempt at resolution, starts to make this an unrealistic certainty. If, as with formal mediation, going to court is involved there is clear risk in this strategy of holding out for the best-case scenario. Even without any possibility of formal proceedings, there is much risk that things could not turn out as you wish if you do not find a resolution.

Worst Outcome

Turning to the worst alternative to an agreed resolution concentrates the mind on what would happen if nothing went your way in the final outcome. Often people involved in a conflict will block themselves from allowing the mind to dwell on a negative outcome. They will shield themselves from the possibility of fault being all theirs, leading to complete capitulation to a situation or the demands of another and recompense for all losses and costs of another also falling to them. This may also seem unrealistic as a certain outcome, but the probability of it being a possible outcome is often enough to fully focus the mind upon achieving a compromised resolution. It is such a bad scenario when considered as a possible reality, emotionally, financially and in terms of a relationship with the other party, that it becomes worthwhile putting a price on avoiding this alternative.

In a conflict which is not going forward to a court case, the risk of these extreme outcomes may not be as pertinent. You may think that because you are not incurring escalating legal costs and are not handing the matter over for third party judgment that there is little risk in not resolving the issue. However, left unresolved conflicts may roll forwards to their own conclusion which may result in an extreme outcome. Therefore, the best-case and worst-case outcomes for your conflict without a current resolution become relevant to you.

Good and Bad Outcomes

Without getting too attached to the specific likelihood at this stage of the best or the worst case, it is good to allow yourself to fully establish simply what each scenario involves. As pointed out earlier, try not to become hooked on the detail when thinking about these scenarios. Rather than becoming either gung-ho about the best case or defeatist about the worst case, try to just envisage each one. If either excitement or hopelessness begin to creep in, remember to take a break and return to broader thinking for a while, to regain perspective.

Once the best and worst outcomes without resolution have been fully formulated in your mind, it is possible to start to look at the reality of each. By delaying the reality test until all positive and negative outcomes have been considered, it will be more realistic and balanced. It is difficult to be objective enough in your own thinking to establish the likely realistic outcome of a conflict situation in which you are actually and probably emotionally involved. However, we usually know quite well what the reality of a situation is likely to be, even if we refuse to overtly consider it, or if we hide it in our subconscious mind.

By allowing yourself to consider the extreme outcomes of a situation, you are likely to get a sense of how likely each is. Even if you are not sure of the realistic outcomes of a situation, the exercise of looking at the extremes might show you something you either want or wish to avoid, maybe even at some cost to yourself. This might be the first time you properly examine what a good or bad outcome would mean for you and how each would really feel to you. Usually, the fear of a chance of the worst outcome occurring, maybe properly accepted for the first time, will be more powerful than the joy at the chance of the best outcome, possibly pondered before.

Example Conflicts and Best/Worst Outcomes

Let us take the first example of a conflict over where to live between a couple. From the point of view of the party favouring a move, the best outcome without current resolution would be an organic decision to make this move, with a suitable purchase property coming along at the right time and a buyer for the current property materialising. It would also be in line with the best outcome if the other person came round to the same way of thinking and was genuinely happy to make this move. If the matter has become a conflict between the two people, how likely is it to really resolve itself by all these things aligning in one person's favour, with no particular effort to bring about a resolution?

In the worst outcome without current resolution for this example, things will just continue the same with one person unhappy in their living arrangements and no change being made. In fact, looking at this situation objectively, it is clear to see that the worst outcome is highly likely for the person who wishes to move without bringing things to an acceptable resolution. By going through the process outlined earlier, it is possible to move from an original position on this conflict. Through considering relevant interests and needs in relation to the issue, it is possible to think of or discuss a resolution which suits both parties to an acceptable degree. There is a lot to lose by doing nothing; it is a risky strategy in this situation. You will come to appreciate this by looking at the reality of the best and worst outcomes for a situation without current resolution and their respective likelihoods. By 'reality testing' the alternatives to facing the issue and resolving it, you will come to see that it is worth the effort it will take to resolve the conflict.

Looking at the second example of conflict, the internal conflict caused by a serious injury, the best alternative to the resolution of the internal conflict is that the injury will miraculously disappear or that it will not affect the person's life in any way. Without considerable effort in finding out how to become better or live well with the injury, it is unlikely that either of these perfect scenarios will occur. The worst case without a resolution in attitude to the injury is that it will progress to a deteriorating life. This can be seen to be a possible outcome if there is no input from conflict management. In deciding to resolve internal conflict regarding the injury, there may be a compromise of fully accepting the limitations caused by the injury but still setting achievable goals in life. This may have the effect of bringing happiness and fulfilment despite the injury. Or the limitations may be accepted to the extent of looking into the medical and alternative treatments which could lead to improvement or recovery. This may involve the compromise of putting work life or life goals on hold for a while, but it might be acceptable to do this if the possible benefits of trying all avenues of treatment have been accepted. These compromised resolutions of internal turmoil can be seen as a better bet than doing nothing and hoping for the best or ending up with the worst.

In the third example of conflict, a workplace conflict for someone who has been passed over for promotion, a lack of current resolution could lead to a best-case scenario of reversal of the decision to promote another, or another opening materialising which grants an equivalent promotion. In the first instance, the scenario looks unlikely without any intervention. In the second case the conflict may continue as there may be ongoing resentment towards the colleague promoted before. The worst-case scenario would be that the status quo leading to the conflict will continue, or it may escalate by further promotion of that colleague or others. The worst outcome could even include being more side-lined than the current position. It may be seen by looking at these options and their real probability of coming about, that an honest discussion with superiors of aspirations and the effect of the current conflict could lead to a better resolution. This person may either be valued in the workplace to the extent that their worth is considered and recognised, or they may discover that they are not valued sufficiently and have the opportunity to place themselves elsewhere, with an appropriate appreciation of worth.

It can be seen from the above examples, that in any conflict situation, considering properly what the best and worst realistic outcomes without a current resolution look like for you, is an enlightening exercise. It is an exercise which will naturally show you the value in making an effort to resolve the conflict. It will reality check the viability of trusting to luck leading to things working out and the real cost of trusting to luck leading to things going badly wrong. The big advantage of conflict resolution, whether formal or informal, is the control you retain over any compromised solution. Taking the decision to put effort into resolution can be an empowering step in itself. Realising how unrealistic a frozen hope for the best is, can focus the mind on activity in the right direction. So too can the realisation of the high risk of a bad outcome from inactivity or not finding resolution now.

Determining Best and Worst Outcomes

Ask yourself the following questions. Take time to think and really imagine the realistic detail of the scenarios. Make notes of the answers you find and notice the feelings which are evoked.

- How good could the outcome to your conflict really be without resolution?

- How bad could the outcome to your conflict be without resolution?

Appreciating fully how bad things could potentially go for you without a resolution is crucial. You may notice a feeling of rising panic as you realise where you could be headed. Having done this work, you may feel a jolt to do all you can to avoid drifting into an unwanted position. This can feel very positive, and you will be ready to look ahead to a brighter future, which is where the next chapter will concentrate your efforts.

CHAPTER 13

Broader Aims

"Fix your course on a star and you'll navigate any storm"
Leonardo Da Vinci

INTERESTS WHICH YOU HAVE, maybe in connection with your conflict, have been covered above but you should extend consideration of your needs to your general life needs and aims. You may have started to think about this with the work you have done to look to the future and now is the time to put more focus on your own life. The conflict in which you are involved is part of your life. Most people are happiest when feeling that there is a positive flow of their life in a direction of their choice.

Blocks to Life and Stress

You may feel that your life aim is to be able to live happily with a contented personal life and a harmonious working life. You may feel driven to have personal or working goals which you would like to achieve. You may feel that moving forwards in life involves cultivating new interests. However you feel fulfilled in life, it is likely that a conflict on any scale which is affecting you will be blocking your life.

The gap between where and how you are now and where and how you wish to be generally in the future is the gap which causes stress. It represents the conflict of things not being the way you want them to be. When reaching this point in the exercise, it is important to look ahead to the future of your life aims and aspirations and not to be pulled into the gap between that and the present conflict. It is better to drop thoughts about the present situation for the purposes of this stage of the exercise, to avoid being lured into too much thought about the gap discussed above. Being side-lined into the stress gap created by the conflict will block your ability to feel fully how you want the future to be and prevent you from feeling just how good your future aims feel. It could be that the conflict situation in which you are in has prevented you from making future plans and thinking about the life aims which sustain us all.

Your Brightest Future

Ask yourself the following questions. Take time to think and feel for the answers and note down your thoughts.

- What does your brightest future look like?

- What would it feel like to be able to achieve this?

By looking toward future aims and assimilating them in your mind, you will be looking at what is important to you. Once this is established, it is useful to look at the aims in connection with the conflict. You will be looking back at the stress gap mentioned earlier, from a perspective of having reinforced the main aims in life. It is now useful to imagine your life without this conflict. Try to imagine other goals, things you could achieve or how you could enjoy the harmony of your life, in absence of the conflict. You will probably start to get a feel for the benefits of being freed from the conflict, not only in terms of the direct issues and relationships involved, but also in whole life terms. Allowing yourself to get a taste of the feeling of freedom from the conflict may start to give you a sense of the real value to you and your life of resolving it.

This is a tool used by professional mediators in bringing about settlement of disputes. It encourages parties with a conflict to focus on movement forward of their lives or businesses, and how better this can be achieved without being hampered by the conflict. By doing this, focus shifts from the dispute to a broader picture of one's life or a company's direction. Perspective of the conflict generally is gained. Usually, the conflict will start to look like a very small part of a much bigger picture. It will also be seen as an irritant to the bigger picture and one which it is not worth being stubborn over. Of course, justice and fairness are still important, but one can start to think in terms of resolving a conflict more readily and maybe in an alternative way to an initial, rigid idea of recompense.

Perspective

Taking an overview and gaining perspective are important parts of any decision-making. It is difficult, especially when working largely on your own to resolve a conflict, to fully gain that perspective. Shifting the focus from the issues of the conflict to the aims of your life should be a useful way to ensure development of the perspective required. It is another way of providing a real reason to yourself for resolving the conflict. Take a moment to reflect and try to notice in what ways your conflict is holding your life back.

Example Conflicts and Blockages they Cause

In the first example of conflict of living somewhere which creates a conflict between partners, it can be seen that instead of proceeding to enjoy all aspects of life, thoughts can get tied up with frustration about the location of residence. If a couple were living in a place agreed by both to be acceptable, how different would life look? What would be the things which time would be spent on? Where would thoughts and mind activity be invested? How would the relationship change without this conflict? These are some of the questions that you could be asking yourself about your conflict.

Thinking of the second example of conflict, an internal conflict created by injury, it is clear that life can get stuck over the inner turmoil. Life can freeze in the sense of not moving forward in any area because the situation is unwanted. How much energy is spent struggling with the fact of the unwanted injury? How much time is wasted being unhappy and frustrated? What other things could be achieved with this energy and time? What would quality of life be like without the conflict?

There is much to be said for contentment and living in the moment without the distraction of conflict, thereby allowing the enjoyment of life. Opportunities, positive changes, achievements and accomplishments will usually flow from a contented environment, free from conflict. The possibility of these things, although sometimes arising from focus and specific endeavour, need not be particularly contemplated or planned; they can often arise organically from the right conditions.

In the third example of conflict, a workplace conflict can often take over a person's life, mainly because of the proportion of time spent at work. The conflict can spill over into general life, causing unhappiness and general discontent. This can affect not only a person's own outlook, wellbeing, and attitude to themselves but also relationships with others even outside the conflict. Irritation, frustration, and stress being present for most of the day due to the conflict can prevent someone from projecting a pleasant and contented aura. Often without recognising it, it is quite possible to become a generally irritated, frustrated, and stressed person generally in relation to the whole of life, due to those emotions from the conflict pervading the personality. This can make someone not only uncomfortable within themselves but also difficult and unpleasant company for others.

Stress and How the Conflict Affects You

It is worth thinking about how you wish to be and feel generally in life and how the conflict is affecting that. How different could the rest of your life be and feel without the conflict?

Generally, people feel happier and less stressed when free from conflict. This does not mean that anyone should try to aim for no conflicts ever arising in their life. That would be just as unrealistic as aiming to never have any stress in one's life. The best way to deal with conflicts or stress of any sort in life is to watch for these things arising, recognise the situations and, when ready, take positive action, such as concentrating on resolving the conflict.

Some conflict, just as with some stress, is healthy in life and brief episodes concentrating on issues creating conflict or stress is natural. This gives one a stronger sense of progression in life once the issues are dealt with. A charmed life never interrupted by conflict, would be a bland life where there is little chance to learn from situations. This could only happen if you lived in a bubble with many barriers to relationships, social contact, risk, and change. A life devoid of these would either be a life with no fun or stimulation, or it would be a life with no appreciation of consequences and effects on others, which would not be desirable.

For these reasons, conflicts which arise in life should not be resented, and neither should dealing with them. Conflicts themselves are worth having just because the resolution of them will always teach us something and move us forward in life, as well as making us appreciate life after resolution all the more. It is often observed that situations come to a head before they dissipate, and active resolution of your conflicts will simply ensure the effective and efficient operation of that process. It is tempting to think "if only it were not for that person, that action or that occurrence, my life would be great." That is a bit like a fundamentally unhappy person thinking that riches will bring happiness; riches may bring some pleasures and erase some problems, but the fundamental unhappiness will still exist. If the thinking that riches brought happiness were correct, there would be no discontented wealthy people. In reality, our mental state may be affected by external circumstances, which act as triggers, but it is not caused by them.

The movement of life will always ebb and flow. Conflicts are opportunities to move past an ebb and continue with the flow, but just as the ocean recedes more before a big wave, so conflicts when resolved, lead to a more forceful forward progression of life. Now you have done this work, hold these thoughts of bright possibilities for the future and removing obstacles to these.

This will help in finding the strength to be empathetic, understanding of others and life situations and to really put effort into resolution of conflicts to progress beyond them in your life. Establishing your aims within the context of the conflict and beyond it is an important part of this process, which we have looked at here. Next, we will look at thought processes in more detail, as there is much thinking needed for the resolution exercise. In fact, the amount of thought, ideas and solutions which need to come from you may be daunting. This is why a closer look at thought process can help to take the pressure off.

CHAPTER 14

Thought Process

"A good decision is based on knowledge and not on numbers"
Plato

WHEN WE ARE DECIDING what we think about a situation, or what outcome we would like from resolution of a conflict, or what our real aims and interests are, things may not be clear. We all have a feel for things in our lives, or instinctive feelings about circumstances, but sometimes these can be strong and other times they can be hard to discover. Instinctive feelings can get lost in too much rational thought. It is possible to lose touch with how we feel about things deep in our bodies, by overthinking. Conversely instinct can overpower rationality if it is not measured by some thought; this is where a knee jerk type reaction occurs. Here I consider conscious and unconscious thoughts, so that you can be aware that some thinking and some relaxing is involved in coming to conclusions. Knowing that solutions do not have to be through forced thought alone can help to reduce the pressure of dealing with a conflict.

Instinct

Our unconscious feel for things and our conscious rationalisation are a complex series of emotions and thoughts which should be balanced in decision-making, to get things right for each of us. When someone is an expert at something, their great knowledge provides them with an instinct which may tell them more than rational thought. This is because there are a very many complex and hidden judgments and conclusions drawn from observation and all the senses which simultaneously go on behind an instinctive feeling. The greater your knowledge and experience in an area, the more accurate your instincts may be, even if you cannot explain the rationale behind them, or break them down into solid reasons for a feeling.

For example, an experienced and accomplished baker may well realise the second a cake comes out of the oven what it will be like when cut. The first instinct of a good baker will probably be right, not just because of gut reaction, but because of the knowledge behind the gut reaction and the way our minds work. The greater the knowledge and experience of that baker, the more accurate their instinct will be. This may be a combination of seeing thousands of cakes at this stage and knowing how the bake proved to be when the cake was eaten. It may be something to do with how it looks and smells. It may be more to do with being very sure of the method or equipment used. Whatever it is, maybe the person cannot break the feeling down, but strongly feels it is right. This instinct is not as random as it might seem; it will be based on knowledge and understanding, even if that cannot be explained.

A scientific and rational approach can be taken, by maybe inserting a skewer to see if it comes out clean when inserted into the cake. This scientific test will probably be right but doesn't rule out problems other than under baking. It is a test which can aid someone who has less experience to rely on and can act as a double check for an experienced baker. So, most people baking will combine their instinct as to whether the cake is ready and whether it will taste good with a more practical test for readiness and pool the conclusions to provide themselves with a level of confidence about the cake.

We are all experts to some extent in dealing with life circumstances and other people. It is something we all have our life to date's experience of. However, some people have lived longer, are more practised at dealing with these things, or have some other way of being good in this area. Our instincts are important and should be taken note of. They should be borne in mind during all thought processes. However, thought process should also be given time to work. In this way we take advantage of our unconscious experience and knowledge and our conscious rational thought. We make up for any deficiency in our instincts by applying conscious thought to the situation. However, we should hold on to the overall instinctive process because it could just add something to our decision-making, which is naturally correct, without us knowing why or how. Instinct could well, conversely make up for deficiencies in rational thought.

As referred to earlier, when considering facts, instinctive feelings and thoughts flowing from these can lead us to consider unknown matters which may well be of relevance to the conflict and otherwise not included in our thought process at all. Remember that unknown matters may be known to you at some level. Respond to instinctive feelings and thoughts by considering whether they might be logically connected or relevant in some way to the conflict and its resolution.

Reason and Logic

One thing to be wary of with initial instincts is that because they are not a result of logical conclusions, there is room for us to mould them. That is, although our thinking mind might want one thing, our subconscious could go for a different thing, maybe for a good un-thought of reason, but maybe also for convenience.

In the first week of a university course, youngsters are looking for friends, company, and a sense of belonging, as they are away from their childhood friends and family. They may usually prioritise reliability and loyalty in their friends but also value a fun-loving nature. Friends before this point may often have been people who they have known over a long period of time, whose background is clear and whose history is known. They may be drawn to others in this new setting very early, in whom they identify a sense of fun, but as time goes by, the judgment and reliability of those people may soon come into question. Sometimes connections are made with others in new environments, where people are thrown together, which seem strong or a good fit at the time, but later when we get to know these acquaintances on their own or over a longer period, the link we have with them seems more tenuous or the fit not as good.

On other occasions connections can be strengthened by knowing someone over increased time. This goes to show that initial instinctive feelings can change over time with observation, added experience and knowledge and can either be reinforced or called into question. This should be remembered during the course of your thought process and when approaching new problems or issues. It should also be borne in mind during relationships and conversations, to allow time for our true and tested feelings to develop during a decision-making process.

Probability

Most of us will apply some logic to a decision which is to be made. This logic will often involve probability. This would not usually be in terms of an exact mathematical calculation of the probabilities of successful outcome with each available option. However, we will instinctively bear in mind the rough probability of a good outcome. Quite often, however, our rough assessment of probabilities can lead to problems.

This is partly because, although there may be a 50:50 chance of one of two options being the one to lead to the desired outcome, the one which doesn't is 100 percent wrong. It is also true that just because there are two choices does not mean that they are both equally likely to lead to the best outcome. It is further the case that some probabilities are objective and calculable, and some are subjective and can only be based on opinion rather than numbers. Even where probabilities are objective, we are partly misled by them because random results can be counter intuitive. This can be seen in the observation of 50 throws of a die; there will statistically probably be a run of the same result for more than two or three throws, but most of us would not predict that if asked to guess random results, because we expect the probability of this happening to be lower than it actually is. Just because a rare event has happened once does not make the probability of it happening again any lower; lightning can indeed strike twice.

Another example of counter intuitive, objective, calculable probability is the number of people statistically needed to be gathered in a room to have two people with the same birthday. If asked to estimate the number needed for a 50 percent chance and 100 percent chance of this happening, most of us would put it higher than it is. Statistical probability dictates that just 23 people are needed for a 50:50 chance of two matching birthdays and 75 people are required to give a 99.9 percent chance of this happening.

Often when assessing probabilities, we ignore the fact that probability does not change, and we look for past patterns to predict the likelihood of future occurrences. If we have flipped a coin five times and heads have come up five times, most of us assume that the probability of another flip coming up as heads is less likely than a tails result at this point. In fact, the likelihood in terms of probability, of heads coming up is, of course, the same after five heads as it was before the run of five heads; it is still 50:50 because the coin has no memory of the last five flips.

Complex Situations

The more complex a decision is and the more things there are to consider which may impact on the best outcome, the more difficult it becomes to use pure logic or instinct about logic to dictate the best answer. Logic of course is good to employ as part of making a decision, along with our instinct for subjective matters, but for all the above reasons, should be exercised with caution.

Even within the corporate world, where business models are formulated with precise logic to achieve maximum efficiency, one mode of operation may be right for one company and totally wrong for another. This will be so because different priorities drive different industries. In the retail of widgets customer preference, price and quality may be the most important considerations, in differing orders of priority, depending on the product. In the supply of a highly technical service, accuracy may take priority over all else. In the same way different decisions will be right for different people, and different decisions will be right for the same people at different times.

Risk Assessment

Often a decision will be based on a risk/benefit analysis. Again, the risk assessment will be different for each person at each point in time. The attractiveness of a benefit will also vary and cannot be easily measured in a rational way. There are often competing interests involved in a making a decision, such as ethics/economics, heart/head, self-interest/welfare of others.

There is an advantage of applying as many strands as possible of objective logic and subjective instinct to any problem in order to come to the right decision for a given person at a given time: there is also a disadvantage. Just as many meetings between many people in a large organisation can ensure the thorough consideration of a decision for the company, the number of meetings, people and ideas generated can also cloud the issue and hamper a clear way forward. In the end someone needs to take the lead and get a feel for the weight to be given to all strands of considerations and thereby make a decision. After due consideration and proper time given to the decision-making process, stepping back and deciding is required. Setting a time to do this is helpful.

Confidence

How far you will trust yourself to make decisions effectively may be down to confidence. You may have made several good decisions in the past and therefore trust yourself on this occasion. If your confidence is low, because of lack of good experience in decision-making or any other reason, give yourself the best chance by following the steps and advice suggested here and before the whole process becomes very boring, or you get lost in circular thought, which can tend to freeze us, determine to make a decision.

In terms of confidence, it is interesting to note that we tend to either be people who feel we are in charge of our own destiny or people who feel at the hands of external events. This nature tends to be reinforced by things going right for autonomous people and by setbacks for fateful people. The nature of a person in this regard is, it seems, unaffected by the opposite. That is to say, setbacks for an autonomous person do not tend to significantly deter them, and achievements for a person who feels governed by external events do not tend to create much more confidence.

It is good to be aware of this, not necessarily to attempt to change our nature drastically, but more to understand and soften it in order to be able to move forward realistically in terms of decision-making within resolution of a conflict. If you feel you are autonomous in personality you may naturally look to the future and anticipate things which may go wrong, for which you need to prepare. If you believe your life is more dependent on external events, try to make a conscious effort to plan for future events as part of your decision-making. Looking to the future and thinking about things that can go wrong is an important part, not just of being organised, but of success. This applies whether operating in a formal, structured arena or a creative more informal one. Finance Directors provide contingencies in their reserves for the possibility of economic downturn: violinists carry spare strings in case one snaps in a performance. A balance should be struck when looking to the future, between anticipating things for which you should prepare and not dwelling upon those things which could go wrong, once identified.

Organising Data

Part of making an efficient and effective decision, is organising the data through which you sift during the decision-making process. Employing written notes and organising them in a way which gives you easy access for retrieval and review will help. The noting down of relevant matters at each stage of decision-making and conflict resolution will relieve the burden on the brain to retain and continually refer back to them. Recording and organising relevant information will also be more likely to be reliable than just hoping that you will realise, remember, and recall pertinent matters at the correct time. If this information becomes too great it will be more of a hindrance than a help, so there is an advantage in keeping things brief and concise and moving on methodically.

An alternative to written notes during the thought and solution-finding process can be the use of diagrams. For some people the brain works faster and makes better connections this way, keeping a flow of thoughts towards a decision. Diagrams should be simple and symbolic; not works of art. The aim is to record thoughts, and this is the main task, leading to the discovering of solutions. Once the mind is distracted from this by the look of the diagrams, the main task risks being sabotaged.

When studying, some students make written notes on subjects, while others record and summarise things pictorially, through graphs, charts, flows, maps, models, tables, pyramids, or trees. This is because some people find it easier to follow, record or recall thoughts recorded through diagrams. It is best

Resolution for Life

to choose the method which aids your own thought process the most and interferes the least with your flow of ideas. Experiment with both if you are not sure which might help you the most. Shapes are useful to represent ideas with related qualities.

Circles, for example can be used for ideas which lead to each other and then back to the start. Circles are also useful for overlapping ideas or ideas contained within other thoughts. Circles are also good for dividing ideas either equally or unequally, as proportions can be clearly seen. This is shown below:

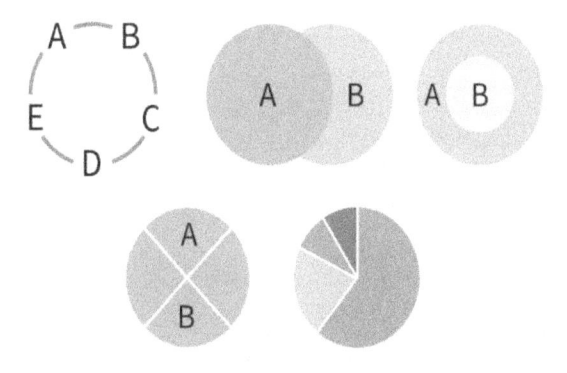

Triangles can show ideas of ascending or descending importance, relevance or preference:

Squares are good for tables of different combinations of ideas, or a list of items combined with items from a different list:

1	2	3	4	5

	A	B	C	D
E	AE	BE	CE	DE
F	AF	BF	CF	DF
G	AG	BG	CG	DG
H	AH	BH	CH	DH

Symbols used can be particular to you and need not conform to any standard model, but there are conventions which help with different processes of thought development.

If you have a central theme with various ideas flowing from or connected to that, a spider diagram can help. Here the central theme is placed in a circle at the heart of the diagram and lines coming out around the circumference of the circle record each related thought. A series of spider diagrams can be created to expand or break down various important issues. Arrows are good to use when one thought leads to another and simple connecting lines can create branches of single or multiple ideas. All these uses of diagram are simple and can be alone or in combination with each other, as seen below:

Spider Diagram

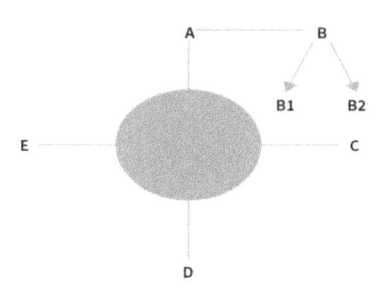

Keeping Perspective

When going through the process of making decisions it is important not to get lost in the detail. In order to keep perspective, you can step back from each strand of thought to see it in relation to other relevant strands. This can be likened to making a mathematical calculation. A good check on the accuracy of arithmetic can be to retain an approximate idea for the plausible upper and lower limits of the calculation. If the maths is undertaken with this in mind, a calculation error is much more likely to be spotted. If the maths is, conversely, undertaken in a bubble with emphasis on the calculation alone and no regard to the ballpark result expected, an arithmetical error can very easily be made.

Step Back and Collate

In decision-making too, it is necessary to step back and to collate, and compare ideas or possible solutions and their likely effect on a situation, given all your knowledge and feel for the issues. This is like a personal quality control function or reality check on the operation of your mind. Usually we perform this function automatically, but when we apply much thought to one area, it is possible to become 'carried away' by possibilities which are unrealistic, so do actively watch out for this. It is the same situation as described earlier, where concentration on detail may need to be dropped for a while to switch your thinking over to a broader view. A break and trying to regain an overview and a reminder of your broader aims within the exercise and generally will help to regain perspective. It will then be possible to return to a focused approach in concentrating on specific strands of thought.

Having looked closer at how we think and make decisions generally may have brought you closer to realising the thought processes which work for you. Bear this in mind as you go forward and as the realisations of the past exercises sink in over time. It is worth revisiting the notes you have made to this point. Re-read them to see if your thoughts have changed, or if a realisation can be triggered. Add any new relevant thoughts to your notes as you go. As communication can be an important part of resolution, that is an area I look at in some detail in the next chapter.

CHAPTER 15

Communication

"Wise men speak because they have something to say; fools because they have to say something"
Plato

IF YOU FEEL COMMUNICATION is needed to resolve an issue, spend some time considering what you wish to say and how best to say it to achieve the required outcome. Some thoughts about how to do this follow. It is always a sound idea to put yourself in the position of the person hearing your words and to imagine the effect on that person. This should ensure that what you say avoids judgment, comparison, or antagonism, which might elicit an un co-operative response.

Judgment / Antagonism

If you wish to avoid judgment, try to ensure that anything which is your view is expressed as an opinion only:

Not: "you are wrong"
But: "I think you are wrong"

Using comparisons may be unhelpful if there is judgment suggested and this can often be the case. For example, "you are just like your mother" used in a negative way is not a statement which will help open communication.

If you wish to avoid antagonism, try not to use the words 'always' or 'never'. If something has happened a few times, say that rather than it always happens. If something is seldom done, again say that rather than 'never'. These definitive words anticipate negative behaviour and may lead to just that. People can feel that there is no point in an effort if it is not expected.

Thinking Ahead

Think about what you want to convey in advance. It is easy to be de-railed once you are bombarded with information. When you meet someone to communicate over an issue, you can lose a sense of how that person is feeling and what their body language gives away, once your brain is overloaded with information, which you will be trying to process and to which you will need to react. Being very clear about what you want to say can help this.

However, there is a balance and you should be wary about not budging from an original viewpoint on things. Often our original thoughts about things can be wrong, but once a thought has been held for a while, it still tends to influence our thinking. If, for example, someone points out a man who they tell you is a thief, and you subsequently learn that they were mistaken in that information, studies have shown that some prejudice towards the person you mistakenly thought was a thief remains. Even when we know we have made a mistake, somehow an element of doubt remains because of our original thoughts.

Listening

There is little point in communication during which you are not prepared to listen and adjust or react appropriately to what is being said by another, as well as deliver your own point of view, thoughts, and feelings. So, it is important to be clear on your own views and points to be made while at the same time being open to another person doing the same and receiving this in a constructive way.

Trust

Be prepared to trust a person with whom you are in communication. There are times when we can be deceived and need to be wary of others but on balance, we gain more from the rapport established through trust than we lose through the risk of deception. Approaching a meeting with your guard up and an atmosphere of suspicion may give you the comfort of preventing being taken in by another, but in fact you may already have lost all chance of having any meaningful communication. It is necessary to sincerely show trust in order to gain the same from another.

If another person approaches us in a closed and guarded way, we tend not to trust them in return. We then find their points of view irrelevant to us and their arguments unconvincing. We tend to become protective and closed as a reflection of their behaviour, which can shut down real communication. It is better therefore to approach a communication with openness and a willingness to trust and to show that trust to the other person. It is more likely that in this way you will establish a meaningful connection and conversation. As a result, there is a far greater likelihood of finding a successful solution to the conflict through the communication. It is in fact in your own best interest to show trust rather than suspicion to move a situation forward.

Emotions

Our faces show our emotions and just as we look at others for clues as to how they are feeling and what they are really thinking, so they look back at us searching for the same. If someone is open and shows surprise and humour in their face, we tend to feel we are dealing with someone who we can understand. If we feel we can translate the language of their face reliably we feel comfortable enough to relax and show our own feelings more freely.

Conversely, if someone sends mixed messages by smiling where there is no humour or retaining a poker face to hide any emotions of surprise, we start to realise that we cannot tell from their face what is really going on with them and we lose trust in what they are saying. We label them as a person we cannot read and we pay less attention to the things they say, because we cannot trust the truth of their words. That is why the court system has developed to require defendants to appear in court for the judge and jury to observe them. It is not just the words they say which are being assessed. Their demeanour while speaking and their facial and bodily reactions to questions and statements are given weight in terms of evidence. If a defendant says "I didn't do it" with a smirk on their face, they are unlikely to be believed. If they make the same denial with an over-earnest look on their face, they may be believed by some but maybe not others. If their words are spoken along with sincere looks and they add open words of explanation, accompanied by appropriate changing facial expressions over a sustained period of time, they are the most likely to be believed.

This shows that if you are wanting the best chance of a good communication, with the other person trusting you and engaging fully with you, you should try to be as natural and open as you can be. If you are prepared to feel this way, it should show in your face; you should allow your emotions to show as they would do normally. Showing our emotions in our face is the way most of us will naturally act; there is nothing extra to do here.

Obviously, a meeting about a conflict can have an acrimonious background and may create a nervous situation, which is normal to feel and again appropriate to show. It would probably raise alarm bells for someone entering into a conversation about a conflict matter with someone looking totally relaxed and at ease. Such an approach would probably appear overconfident or give the impression of not taking the matter seriously. So, be prepared not to hide the natural emotions you feel as they arise, from showing in your face as they normally would, including being nervous. This is not something to overthink.

It is not necessary to try to perfect your facial expressions. In fact, if you try to be different to your normal self in the reactions you reveal, you will achieve the opposite effect. If the other person knows you and your demeanour is different from your usual self, this will create mistrust. If the person does not know you, it will still probably come across oddly if you try to react in a way you wouldn't usually. The best preparation for how you present yourself in a communication, to establish trust, is to be yourself and to allow yourself to feel and react fully in line with that. It is worth going one stage further than allowing your expressions to show your emotions. Be aware of your expressions, without being self-conscious but also be prepared to explain your expressions.

Facial Expression

Facial expression is important because it gives a clue as to how we are feeling to others, and we receive clues back about how they are feeling. It is worth remembering, however, that this is just what facial expression is: a clue. It is better to also voice what you are feeling in order to avoid the doubt of being misinterpreted. One person's surprised face can be another's baffled face.

A strong facial expression can be taken to be a gesture of ridicule. If you are surprised, confused or dumbfounded, it is a good idea to clearly say that that is how you are feeling. It is likewise a good idea to ask for clarification from the other person of what an expression might mean. If another person is frowning, that could well indicate surprise, confusion, disagreement or sadness. It is a good tactic in keeping communication clear to ask for a facial expression to be explained.

If you can see a reaction to something you have said but are not sure what the other person is thinking, it is a good idea to say just that, taking care to sound inquisitive while doing so. It is also good to ask for confirmation even when you think you do know what an expression means. Each emotion which we interpret from another causes a chain reaction in ourselves, so being clear about the emotions and connected signals which are being given out and received is vitally important in keeping communication on track. How many times after the heat of an argument do we return to dissect the exchange with the other and realise that an expression was misinterpreted midway through the exchange which escalated feelings on both sides? It is best to be transparent about your own feelings as you feel them arise: to show them and explain them. It is also good to be prepared to watch for changes in the other person's emotions which they show and to clarify them too as they come up.

Anger

A proviso to being yourself and expressing your emotions is to keep anger under check. Feeling anger and showing this in your expression or explaining the emotion is not necessarily a bad thing, but not to the extent of allowing anger to take over.

Anger is an emotion which can quickly escalate, transfer back and forth and express itself physically. If voices become raised step back from the communication. Take a moment to re-compose yourself. We are all used to controlling anger as socially appropriate. By exercising control, your behaviour should be reflected by the other person. If you become aware that the other person has escalating anger step back further to allow cooling off time either within, or if necessary, away from the conversation. While honesty over feeling angry and a certain amount of venting of emotions can be helpful, an atmosphere of increasing anger will do nothing towards achieving resolution.

This seems like very obvious guidance of which we are all aware. However, the difference between awareness of the unacceptability of showing too much anger and a definite intention to avoid showing open anger during communication is enough to warrant drawing attention to it specifically. It is worth forming the intention to avoid a situation of escalating anger in advance of a conversation. After all, we have probably all had conversations which begin in an innocuous manner and end up in a heated argument; when looking back we are not sure how things went from the start point to the end point. This often happens when we are unprepared for a topic or certain emotions. Being fully prepared for a communication with intention to keep it within certain parameters goes a long way to ultimately keeping it under control.

Public or Private Space

The place chosen for the communication to happen is important. It should usually be somewhere private, where you are not concerned about being observed or overheard. However, there may be circumstances where you prefer the meeting to be in a public but impersonal place, or for a known person or persons to be present. If that is the case these details should be agreed in advance and all people should be comfortable with the arrangements. It would be good to agree what role any other people will play; whether they are just there as observers and for support or whether they will be invited to comment at all.

All distractions should be excluded as far as possible and mobile phones should all be switched off before the discussion begins. It usually helps to find some neutral territory for the discussion, which does not give more or less ease to one person, unless there is a place where both people feel equally comfortable and is not itself emotive to the subject matter of the conflict. Both people involved should agree on the venue and it should be checked in advance that they are both comfortable with the place.

In formal mediations, the venue is often arranged by the mediator, who will have access to or hire a series of quiet meeting rooms away from the premises of either party. Sometimes hotel facilities are used. Food can sometimes be included if the discussions run over a mealtime; sandwiches are usual as they are easy to handle, do not require much focus and can be left to eat later if discussions are in mid flow.

Alcohol is not a good idea, even in an informal setting. The likelihood is that both people will be nervous, and the discussion will be important and require concentration. A Dutch courage pre-meeting drink, drink during discussions to relax everyone, or a celebratory drink when things appear to be going in the direction of agreement may seem acceptable, but it is better to decide before a meeting to avoid alcohol. Our judgment, ability to focus while retaining thoughts about the future, to adhere to an agenda of important items, to speak and listen at the appropriate times and to read another's emotions will all be affected by alcohol. It is easy to have a discussion in everyday life which you look back on and wish you had said something different or picked up on something small at the time, so it is best to keep your senses as keen as they can be.

Communicating the Facts

The content of what you say will be vital. As outlined before, facts are an important starting point for looking at issues of conflict. It is important not only that you are objective in stating the facts but also that you confirm the other person's understanding of what has happened. Try to state facts without making comments on what has happened to begin with. Simply try to summarise what has happened, which should be agreed. Also be aware of giving too much information, which could cloud the matters being raised; try to be succinct and to stick to relevant information only. You may have to edit the content of what you wish to speak about in advance in order to achieve this.

Once there has been some agreement on facts, an open and potentially collaborative atmosphere may have been established. There will at the very least have been the greatest chance of this happening. From there communication should turn to how you have been affected by what has happened. Try to explain this in a way which remains non-judgmental as outlined above. Judgment can be avoided here by stating how things have been or felt to you and not by stating what you think about what has happened. How you have been affected includes emotionally, financially, physically or in any other way you feel. Try not to apportion blame for how you feel or what has happened, as this will not create a collaborative atmosphere. It is important to take personal responsibility for things that you have done or said and also for how you feel. Events and actions of others can trigger reactions for you but will rarely be the sole cause when it comes to your feelings.

Communicating Your Needs

The next plan for any communication will be to communicate your needs. Needs have been dealt with in Chapter 10, where we established that your specific and general needs over this conflict and in wider life should be identified. Needs should be clearly stated in any communication, so think about how you can effectively and efficiently state your needs. Remember to think about how your words will be received and to avoid antagonism.

Finally, think in advance about what you want from the other person. Be prepared to go into a conversation with a request in mind and think about the language you will use to make your request clear. If you are simply aware of what you don't want and not sure about what you do want, you are unlikely to get whatever it is that you actually want. It is insufficient to explain how you feel without going on to clarify what you want in straight forward terms. If you make a request, there are four possible responses:

1. Refusal.
2. Silence.
3. Bargaining.
4. Acceptance.

In the case of a flat refusal, it is always possible that the door has been opened to a wider thought on the part of the other person. Your communication and requested solution may well be thought about over time and lead to bargaining or even acceptance.

If your communication is met with silence, the above is again true. It may seem that communication has been impossible, but if your words have been heard, they may well lead to positive thoughts, actions, and resolution in the future. Unless the other person literally puts their fingers in their ears and says "La, la, la" there is hope!

In either the case of bargaining or outright acceptance of your request, your communication has been immediately successful. Often a face-to-face conversation, stating clearly, calmly, and honestly the conflict situation you are in and a reasonable solution that would suit you, will be positively received. Most people have some empathy with almost anyone if they are honest, clear, and non-antagonistic in their approach. It is not even always necessary to agree with someone to acknowledge how things have affected them. There may be differences between you, but a resolution may still make both people feel better. There may be disagreement but also sympathy for another. There may be no agreement but still there may be acceptance. These situations allow resolution.

Don't Demand, Empathise

Care should be taken to ensure that a request does not come across as a demand. This is not always about the phraseology of what is said but also about the response to any answer. It is important to try to empathise with the other person before trying to persuade compliance with your request. This empathy has a dual role; firstly, it is more likely to secure the immediate success of any persuasion and secondly, it can lead to a later more successful resolution. The reason for this is that the other person will expect an empathetic response in future. If there is a resigned negative response to a request, that will be remembered. Phrases such as "I knew you'd say that" or "you always do this" tend to set a pattern of expected negativity and illicit both immediate and future stubbornness in the other person.

There is a further aspect of empathy which can move us further towards resolution of a conflict and that is the act of seeing things from the point of view of another. When dealing with your own established view of a situation, you will naturally have created a narrative based around yourself. If you have discussed the situation with friends and family, they will probably have supported and reinforced your own given opinions on the issues, as it is human nature to agree and support those we identify with. It is therefore a good exercise in objectivity and broad thinking to begin to empathise with another person.

Concentrating on this empathy is also an effective method of dealing with the natural bias we all have against anyone with differences to us. Although we can rationalise this bias and attempt to exclude it, however broad minded and accepting we feel we are, social experiments show that we are inherently driven by psychological principles to agree with those with whom we identify, to adjust our behaviour to align with those we see as our social group and to hide behind accepted group norms in terms of responsibility. In other words, most of us will consider that if someone we respect and identify with thinks or acts in a certain way, it is alright for us to do the same. As social psychologists J. Darley and B. Latane point out, we collectively accept societal norms. We are more likely to persuade those who are outside the group we identify with of our own view, than to try to align ourselves with the view of someone who disagrees with us and is outside the group we identify with. Thus, developing empathy for someone who represents opposition is an exercise in softening the natural bias which can impede conciliation.

Sometimes people worry that showing sympathy with another's thoughts, feelings or actions where there is a conflict with that person, reveals weakness or a loss of bargaining power. This way of thinking, where there is a fear of admitting wrongdoing is highly defensive and legalistic. It is best to avoid a legal-type approach when trying to resolve conflicts informally. Where a legal case is mediated before going to court, the discussions of the mediation are confidential and without prejudice; that is, they may not be brought up later if the case proceeds to court. The reason for this is to ensure that all parties can honestly and sincerely communicate with each other without fear of incrimination and without the need to point score. Try to ensure that some such atmosphere of freedom is created in your communication.

Equality

When a decision is made to communicate with another over a conflict, thought should be given in advance to any inequalities between yourself and the other person. A mediator's role would encompass evening out any imbalances in power, status or experience and also in understanding or communication skills. If, on consideration you believe the other person to be disadvantaged in equality, then allow more time for digestion of your words, slow the pace, and explain more in straight forward terms. Think of your appearance and avoid over dressing. Try to make the other person comfortable, remembering that it is in your interest to set as advantageous an environment as is possible, to achieve resolution. If, on the other hand, you feel at a disadvantage and it is you who feels uncomfortable or disadvantaged in equality, maybe be prepared to say how you feel and ask for what you feel is necessary to achieve a more level platform. For example, do not hold back from asking for clarification or a slower pace.

When preparing to speak to another person about a conflict, as well as having an agenda of the things you would like to outline, explain, and ask for, think also of the other person and allow them to do the same.

This is achieved by listening to their words with attention which requires you, during their time of speaking, to empty your mind as far as possible. When another person is speaking in the context of a conflict, by trying in that moment to connect their words to your own requirements you will distance yourself from properly listening and being on the same wavelength as that person. Allowing yourself to listen fully, leaving behind your own standpoint is important. It is tempting to think that you will lose the strength of your argument or the focus of your desired outcome by doing this, but in fact you are very much more likely to achieve your aim in resolution if you are prepared to listen in this way. The reason this helps is that doggedly following the intellectual logic in your own mind blocks your empathy. By allowing space for empathy towards another, you will also allow the best chance of this being felt by them and reflected towards you at some stage.

Look Beyond and Evaluate

Further to listening properly you can go a step further and look behind the other person's words for their explanations and needs. While someone may outline things from their perspective and make requests of their own, there may be reasons and requirements implicit in what they are telling you or you may have to ask further to clarify these. Try to look for what a person needs rather than what they think. They will have to go through the process you have been through in moving from positions to interests. If they have not made this transition, you may have to encourage them to do so or to actively participate in the process for them. Having completed the exercise yourself, you should be in a good position to help. It is not a selfless exercise to do this; an acceptable resolution is likely to come from the practice of this. It is also more likely that the other person will feel less threatened if you hear their needs, rather than their thoughts and this environment is conducive to resolution.

Another thing to watch for is that what another person says might not be what they think either consciously or subconsciously. You will need to follow a conversation and regard any relationship which exists with intuition, backed by experience of this person or people in general. Intuition is useful to us, especially in complex situations when pure logic with many threads can lead to different conclusions and much thought can lead to confusion. This may be the reason why Sigmund Freud advocated important decisions being made from the unconscious.

Being intuitive is however difficult under stressful circumstances. You need to be careful to put yourself in the mind-set of the other person and to keep your emotions in check. If you are thinking wholly from your established point of view this may block picking up on feelings of the other person. Whilst a little stress can serve to improve our overall focus, extreme emotions which cause the heart rate to race too high can also preclude us from noticing the small things about another person's demeanour which give us intuitive clues.

The reason for this is that when we are in fight, flight or freeze mode our focus is narrowed to concentrate on what the body thinks it may need to do to respond to the cause. The body's response to a perceived physical threat (which a very elevated heartbeat does represent) is to shut down any functions which are subsidiary to the main function of fighting, running away or playing invisible. In extreme cases this can block peripheral vision hence the phrase 'blind rage'. It can also serve to block sound and affect perception of reality; thus, the description of those in great fear often seeing things in slow motion or finding themselves watching a scene which appears to have gone silent. You may stop noticing nuances and fall back to relying upon the established thought pattern you have about the situation or person, which has perpetuated the conflict. This is unhelpful.

Avoid losing your valuable sense of watching the other person, picking up on clues they give and accurately judging things by slowing everything down if you feel your heart racing; pause, leave gaps, and take time to think. This will avoid 'knee jerk' reactions which represent a snap response to an instant feeling which may not be your balanced or best reaction to the same situation.

When we respond too quickly to a sudden emotion we often look back and regret this with hindsight; the only thing which has changed our mind is often the passage of time. Another useful thing to do is to practise what you wish to say in advance and try to anticipate responses which could cause heightened anger or anxiety. There is no need to obsessively cover every possible response but some rehearsal in this way can help maintain calm and from that, perspective during the conversation. In turn this tends to keep intuition flowing.

You can also make sure you are observing the other person in a balanced way and not overly focusing on any one thing they are doing: this could be described as listening with your heart and not your eyes. Overly focusing, say on a nervous tick which the other person has, may start to take over in your mind as an incorrect clue to untruthfulness. Furthermore, try not to lose overall balanced focus by relying on your preconceptions.

For example, be sure that what you translate as a shifty look, which you would usually not trust, is not actually a squint which cannot be helped. It can also be helpful not to over think things while in conversation. If you try to explore every logical avenue of your argument at this time, the points you are making will take over in your mind from your general feel for the situation: too much information can block intuition. Again, we come back to the point that our intuitive judgment can be invaluable and should be allowed proper time and space within situations such as this. The time-honoured advice to 'sleep on it', referred to earlier, where an important decision is to be made underlines the fact that our educated subconscious can be better at understanding the best way forward, and this often happens when the mind is not actively following threads of reasoning. In order to listen and judge the situation fully, it is best to make your points succinctly and try to retain composure and balance from there.

With the above in mind, balanced and controlled intuition can help you greatly. If you get a feeling that someone is not speaking the truth (knowingly or unknowingly on their part) you are probably right and should probe further in a gentle way, which might break down barriers to honest communication. In this case try to evaluate what has been said and to challenge it non-aggressively.

Reflecting Back

A good communication skill and one used by mediators throughout a mediation is reflecting back what is being said by paraphrasing. This will lead to confirmation of your understanding of what the other person is saying, or it will elicit further clarification where your understanding is not correct. This tactic has a further role of allowing time for the other person to revisit what they have said and to reinforce it (or otherwise) in their own minds. Only paraphrase where it is appropriate for sympathy or understanding and take care with the tone used otherwise it can be aggravating. Paraphrasing may be useful where language becomes highly charged, in order to filter out negative emotion and to distil it to the need behind it, but equally there is usually sensitivity associated with strong emotion, so tact is called for. Generally paraphrasing used well will save time and avoid misunderstandings or wrong avenues in communication.

Another tactic familiar to professional mediators is that of allowing those in a conflict to vent. Take care to allow the other person to fully express their view, thoughts, and feelings before trying to move too quickly on. Rushing towards resolution will be counterproductive because if both parties have not had the opportunity to vent their emotions, they will rarely be ready in terms of calmness, empathy and ultimately concession, to resolve the issue satisfactorily. You will usually be able to tell when tension has been fully released through the other's words as they will naturally come to a halt. This underlines the need to allow space to listen properly.

The whole listening process can only happen effectively if we resist the urge to comment or advise when another person is explaining their viewpoint and feelings. Remember to leave silence for the person to fully speak and for empathy to develop. If you yourself are too emotional to feel any empathy, you should address this, maybe by mentioning the strength of your feelings and the fact that you are aware that this is blocking empathy. You should also consider that many of our needs as people are the same and this can bring an understanding of another's needs, which in turn can explain actions or lead to solutions.

If you are feeling primarily judgmental, this will impede resolution. It is worth getting yourself to a position in which you are empathetic, because doing this means you are more able to receive empathy from another; this flows from the feeling of empathy you have and show towards that person. This is part of establishing an atmosphere of mutual respect within which to communicate and this is important in achieving resolution of the conflict. Furthermore, you are unlikely to be able to assist in moving the process successfully towards resolution in this state, as you will not be in the correct frame of mind in which to draw out the needs of another and identify their interests.

Focus

Focus will be important during communication, and this is best maintained by remaining in the present. Although this may seem obvious it is something which we do not easily do naturally. Most people's minds will dwell on the past and race into the future, both within themselves and while they are communicating. Although there may be discussion about past events and future aims, the solution will happen only in the present moment. Extend being present enough to listen and to be consciously present when speaking.

If when communicating, you are making an effort to be sympathetic, focused on the present and listening to the other person, you have a good chance of this being returned. However sometimes the other person has not yet reached this stage and is still blocked by anger or judgment themselves. If you are met with such a response, you should try to understand the reasons for the strong emotion. If you can guess at this, or ask about it and have an honest discussion, this may move things forward.

There may be times when you would like a meeting with someone and are ready to communicate but they refuse. This can be frustrating, but a start can be made by writing down what you would have said, or maybe record yourself saying it. You will have to guess at the feelings and needs of the other party, but maybe by doing so you can hit upon something which they may be relieved for you to bring up. You can send the record of your points and thoughts arising about the issue to the other person. Use all the skills set out above and try to show empathy and respect in the spirit of resolution.

One cautionary word about seeing things from another's point of view and using empathy is not to go so far as to presume how another will act or what another wants. People are complex and even when we think we know someone well they can act unpredictably at times. We often even get our assessment of ourselves wrong and look back in hindsight at decisions which could have been different. So, trying to second guess another's likely decision is unhelpful. Looking at the type of solutions which might work for them, what we might do in their situation, or what a person with their personality, attributes and situation might wish to do could be helpful preparation for communication but you should not get carried away with assumptions.

When you come to communicate with a person, try not to think that you can sum them up through a conversation. It is not reliable to get a feel for how you think someone will act and to rely on that. As mentioned, trying to assess how another person is feeling and how they are responding to you is an important part of communication but waiting to hear their actual response and solidifying mutual ideas and agreements is also important. It is vital to formalise any agreements about issues or concurrence about future actions or resolution, as will be dealt with in Chapters 17 and 18.

Be prepared for this formalisation of detail to be part of a conversation. Once you move away from a communication, much can change for many reasons. Feeling a connection with someone through communication, seeing their differences to you, gaining an understanding of someone, and looking them in the eye while agreeing certain action are all important points, but not sufficient to rely on in securing actual resolution.

People can send intentional or unintentional misleading signals, they can change their minds, other things can happen quickly to influence them in another direction. Be prepared to focus on each moment of the communication and to focus on the detail of the ideas and agreements which arise and securing their practical accomplishment. Use interpersonal skills but do not allow them to lead you to presumption. Remember to be broad minded and accepting, listening to what is being communicated to you and being prepared to adapt to it, while holding the points of importance for you as central to discussions. If you are utilising communication as part of your resolution, chances are this is a conflict with someone where the relationship matters to you. If you have strong feelings for the person with whom you are in dispute this can be an advantage, which I look at next.

CHAPTER 16

The Advantage of Love

"In love our problems disappear"
Sir Paul McCartney - Pipes of Peace

IF THE CONFLICT YOU have is in a relationship of familial, romantic or good friendship love, you have a big asset on your side. By concentrating on the love that exists in a relationship you can shift the focus of importance away from the conflict issues. I encourage you now to think about the relationship if someone else is involved. It is worth thinking about the history of the relationship and how love has grown. Remind yourself of that.

Firstly, consider these questions:

- What are the events and actions that have existed to build a close relationship?

- How have you felt about the person concerned in times of affection? Try to access that feeling in order to ensure you are approaching the conflict from that standpoint.

- Think also about the future of the relationship and the nature of the love. How will the conflict affect this?

- How do you wish the future relationship to be?

Example Conflicts and Close Relationships

Taking the first example of conflict over where to live, this is likely to be a conflict with someone with whom there is love. It is easier to see another's standpoint if there is a close relationship, built over time. There is likely to be understanding about the background of that person, what makes them tick and what their needs are. They may wish to live in a certain location because that is what their family accepted, what they are used to and what they feel comfortable emotionally with replicating. Conversely, they may want to live in a location because it is the opposite to what they have known in their family, and they wish to go in a different direction for specific emotional reasons. Naturally, either way, this must be balanced against the other's needs and wishes, but broad thinking is easier when there is love as a historical background and love as a reason to resolve a conflict for the future. In this example it will be in a person's interest to resolve the living location conflict because they will wish to live happily with the loved one.

If, as in the second example of an injury, the conflict is internal, love for oneself is key. We are told from so many sources that all love sprouts from high self-regard and without that, growing any other sort of love is hard. It can be a difficult thing to cultivate if it has not grown naturally from childhood and in that case, it will take time to establish, like any other love. Thinking of oneself as another person to be considered in any situation can help. If considering a friend in the same situation, instead of themselves, how would that person act or feel? Even if there is a healthy level of self-regard within a person it is worth reminding oneself of its importance. When a life changing event occurs, such as a serious injury, it is possible to forget the self in the turmoil of the conflict. Maybe there is a dogged determination to maintain the status quo of one's life, without regard to wellbeing. Maybe there is an overwhelming anger which overrides the urge to care for oneself. If the internal conflict is something that has gradually arisen, it may be that the self has been forgotten gradually along the way until there is little care on a practical level. In any case it is important to nurture love for yourself in order to resolve any internal conflict.

In the last example of a work problem, there may be compassion, empathy and understanding for others in the workplace which is important. Love is easier to access when the relationship is one of a family, romantic or friendship bond, but a type of love can be felt for others, especially acquaintances or work colleagues, or even for strangers. There are parts of all of us that are the same, which is why we can sympathise and empathise with others. When you have any knowledge of the history of a person this can be more easily accessed. It is possible to connect to this feeling for strangers, if you forget the conflict for a moment and see yourself as just two beings, breathing and living in a big world.

Find Common Ground

Where the conflict is with another who is in this category, try to find some common ground. In the short time in which I was involved in criminal law it was rarely that I interviewed or was party to a conference with a person accused or convicted of a crime, even a hardened person, or a heinous crime, where I could find no spark of human empathy. Sometimes it was sympathy with circumstance or some part of a person's life, sometimes it was being moved by a situation or position in life and other times it was an understanding of some part of a person's actions, even where they were wrong, or I didn't agree with them.

Finding this connection with someone with whom you are in conflict is in itself a spark of love or humanity. Try to find and work upon that spark. Thinking about the conflict with a feeling of some empathy for a person, even if it exists outside the conflict, may change the focus of your thoughts. All this is really, is putting yourself in another's position, but that is easier for some than others and quite difficult for anyone when clouded by the emotions of a conflict. People are said to be blinded by anger, but equally they are said to be blinded by love. The former type of blindness narrows us in a damaging way, whereas the later shields us from injury.

Try this Exercise:

Shut your eyes and think about something that makes you angry; feel the effect on your body. Now think of a situation of love; feel the difference in your body. It is kinder to yourself to feel love for others; it is not a selfless thing, there is a huge personal benefit.

Don't Over-Compromise

One thing to look out for with conflicts in a relationship of love is any tendency to over-compromise. Because the situation is one where we are invested in the relationship and are aware of ongoing ramifications of uncomfortable issues we raise, we can sometimes be very keen to achieve resolution. This resolution should not be at any cost. It is important to stand certain ground, to identify important points and issues for you and to keep those in mind during conflict management. If you concede or ignore issues which are important to you for the sake of making peace within an ongoing relationship, there may be problems further down the line. Resolution may be achieved but this may be only on a superficial level where unhappiness and resentment still remain, even if supressed for the time being. Those feelings will resurface. If there are strong feelings causing conflict within a relationship, these need to be aired and not ignored if a true resolution is to be achieved.

Take care not to be scared to raise issues causing a real conflict for you in an effort to avoid discomfort to another. It is possible to be honest and open about things another does or a status quo between you which causes unhappiness for you. Even if the other person will find this revelation painful or surprising. If you sincerely want a continued relationship free from conflict, some difficult things may need to be said. This may take some courage and may well seem to increase conflict by causing difficulty for the other person initially. However, your conflict is just being aired and thereby equally shared; not actually increased. Protecting another from discomfort and bearing all the difficulty yourself is neither fair nor healthy for the relationship and it is not any way to resolve a conflict.

With the sort of situation where the other person may be unaware, purposely ignoring or in denial of a problem for you, communication will be necessary. The best ways of communicating are covered in Chapter 15. In this instance staged communication may be necessary, where you gently introduce the conflict topic and then allow time for any raw emotion, surprise or resentment to subside before attempting further communication with the aim of leading to resolution. This allows the other person time to calm down, think and approach the issue both rationally and from the heart, rather than in a knee jerk reaction way.

Dominance

Usually, one person will be more dominant in certain areas of a relationship, and you should look out for this affecting the resolution. It may be your issues, or alternatively matters important to another in a close relationship, which should be given more consideration, in order to equalise any imbalance in reaching resolution. Whether the dominance in certain areas is on the other person's side or on your side, you should try to consider whether this is happening and any concerns you have regarding balance should be raised to bring this into the open, during resolution discussions.

It is good to have tapped into your feelings for another involved in a conflict, or indeed for yourself. It is important to stop the thinking for a bit in order to fully realise the emotions you feel and the effects on your body in terms of relationships. You should now be well equipped with thoughts on yourself, your conflict, others involved and the skills of decision-making, communication and using positive emotion. Also using notes on exercises completed at each stage of the process, you are close to being able to access a resolution. We will look at this final stage now.

CHAPTER 17

Resolution

"Happy the man who has been able to learn the causes of things"
Virgil

I HAVE SHOWN YOU how to prepare for the resolution process and the benefits to you of finding a resolution. Remind yourself of these things and maybe recap on Chapters 2 and 3 at this point. You will have thought about and noted your position on the conflict, the facts, the history, and the future of the conflict. You have gone through the stage of reality testing the strengths and weaknesses of your position and moved towards your needs and interests. By looking at the likelihood of a good outcome and the worst that could happen without resolution you will have a balanced view of the worth to you of resolution. This is re-enforced by the consideration of your broader life aims and what a general bright future looks and feels like to you. With the addition of thinking about decision-making, communication and the specific emotions of the relationship you are well placed to find a resolution, which I discuss more here.

Completeness

Make sure your search for solutions is full and try to include any unknown workable solutions. Try not to dismiss possible solutions freshly occurring to you as not possible. As mentioned earlier, try to consider unknown solutions, in line with Rumsfeld's thinking. Remember that unknown solutions may be both known at some level or totally unknown to you. Really this whole exercise is usually about uncovering the solution which you knew about at some level but had not realistically realised as a practical resolution. The resolution exercise can uncover latent knowledge which comes to the fore with a little work and intentional focus. Alternatively, it could be about coming to a solution which you did not know about at all before. Maybe at the start of the conflict resolution process you knew that you did not know the solution. You may have already given considerable thought to the solutions which have always occurred to you as a possibility, and if they have not up until this exercise lead to resolution, then new ideas may be necessary. Do not be put off resolution by dismissing a novel idea for a solution, just because it does not look the way you thought it would.

Parameters

If you are finding a conclusion hard to come to it can help, once the necessary time has been applied to the exercise generally, to give yourself a time parameter within which to work. If you have allowed enough time for full and varied thought as set out above, you can give yourself a deadline for sifting through the strands of embryonic solution and formulating a final resolution. This has the advantage of stopping circular thought, which can occur if too much leeway is given at this stage. It is generally not a good idea to limit the general consideration time which comes before this stage, but once this has been properly allowed for, there can be an advantage in limiting the time for your mind to go round in circles.

Overthinking

Once a solution occurs to you which could work, try to give it the benefit of the doubt in so much as not overthinking it. If a solution feels right, it probably is. Adding too many alternatives and options through extra thought about how this solution could work may just serve to confuse the mind and cloud the exercise. If you have put in the broader thinking work and thought around the conflict sufficiently, you should trust that a solution which occurs to you now has good chances of success. During formal mediations, once an agreement is reached between parties, a mediator will be keen to enshrine it in a written agreement, to capitalise on the flow of positivity for resolution. Often leaving things - even matters which seem certainly settled - until the next day can risk agreements being wide open to changes of heart. Be bold and commit yourself to a solution which seems right. Resolve to put it into action.

That is not to say that a solution which occurs to you may not need just a little extra work. It may need to be added to or combined with something else in order to represent a full and wholly workable solution.

Putting a Resolution into Action

Once you have a solution make sure you think through the practical details of it. When and how will it be put into action? Many a formal mediation has fallen apart after resolution because the agreement is not specific enough. Professional mediators know that leaving wriggle-room for further disagreements and delays in seeing through a resolution can be fatal to final settlement. Put the last bit of effort into this exercise at the right time, before you go off the idea, or persuade yourself that it will not work. Do not allow time for old patterns of thought to re-emerge around the conflict.

If there is another person involved in a conflict, there is twice the chance that things seemingly agreed may evaporate when you part ways after communication. The other person may discuss things with someone else and have a change of heart. They, as well as you, may return to old ways of thinking when left to their own devices. This might be more likely for the other person if you have initiated communication. It is probable that they have not put in as much work on broad thinking and real movement from position to needs and interests as you have done, in advance. This means that they may have had a shift sufficient to agree in person on a resolution, but this is not reinforced by work done earlier, and they could more easily be derailed. As the examples of a conflict between a couple on where to live and a workplace conflict are both likely to involve another person, the above considerations are relevant: these examples are examined further below.

Example Conflicts and Action Plans

In the first example of conflict where there is conflict between a couple on where to live, some agreement should be set when a resolution has been reached to cement agreed points. Maybe there has been discussion around preferences of living location of each person, their background reasoning and feelings and the way in which decisions are arrived at as between the two people. This is all good conciliatory work, which can resolve the conflict with a specific plan, but without this nothing may change in the conflict area. There should be a mutual agreement on how to make decisions in a more balanced way in future. Further to this, it is preferable to carry through from the discussion discoveries to a timely and solid agreement about the specific conflict and a particular location. Agreeing that there are compromises needed and accepting another's point of view may resolve a conflict in terms of present feelings, but in order to prevent the conflict re-emerging in a similar or even a different form, specific points should be confirmed at this stage.

In the second example of conflict, where there is inner conflict over an injury, the resolution a person concerned may have come to is likely to be a personal plan. It is more likely to be a solution that is borne from realisations about themselves and maybe some determinations to make personal changes. This is an easier resolution to finalise detail of, in many ways, if only that person's ideas and decisions need to be crystallised.

By way of illustration, maybe the injury caused conflict because the person originally felt that it had prevented them from having a very active social life, which they sought. It could be that they have realised during this process that a very active social life does not, and maybe never did, accord with their preferences. Their resolution may be to do less socially and to worry less about that. The solution needs to go further at this stage, to make sure that it is carried through successfully into that person's life. It may be necessary for them to make a list of prioritised social engagements and a list of things which will be cancelled or not arranged. It may be necessary to have conversations with friends and family about the things to be cut out and the reasons for the eliminations.

Without these specifics being firmed up, it might be that the person will be lured into old habits of accepting unsuitable social engagements or being offered invitations to unrealistic activities which they feel bad about declining. So, the work done in reaching a realisation in this area of life, and a decision about the future which will erase the conflict could easily be overridden, without a set and detailed plan of action. This plan is part of the resolution and should be drawn up now. Setting the plan in writing can help to follow it up as there may be things which cannot be done instantly.

If this is the case, a timescale should be set. For example, this weekend a list of planned events, appointments or activities will be cancelled. By the end of the following week a conversation with a spouse and a good friend will be had to explain the situation and the likely effect on planned activities. After that there will be a reaction carried through on receipt of a social engagement offer or on consideration of social activities, firstly deciding priority and secondly considering that priority within the context of current physical ability and the injury. Agreeing this plan with themselves will make that person more likely to avoid future conflict in this area and reap the true rewards of the resolution exercise.

In the third example of a workplace conflict, a person may decide to resolve a conflict over not receiving a past promotion by working towards a future one. The ways in which this will be achieved should be formulated now. A woolly idea to acknowledge current lack of experience, do good work and be promoted in six months may not have the desired conclusion. This could lead to further conflict, a feeling of wasted effort and a greater sense of lack of control over the conflict. The conflict may have involved a peer who has received a promotion or a superior responsible for promotions. If there has been communication with these people as part of the resolution process, an agreement with them should now be made. This may be an informal spoken agreement, for example, to be treated with respect as a person working towards the same level as another employee. Alternatively, it may be a more formal written commitment to consider that person for the next promotion if certain target tasks are achieved in the meantime.

Final Detail

Try not to become too distant from the thinking of the exercise and the strands of varied thought work which have gone into finding a solution. Apply yourself to the final detail of how the solution will look to you and anyone else concerned. If it helps, you can write this down to keep yourself on track and remind yourself, and any other person involved, later of why this solution seems right now and exactly what steps are necessary to carry it out.

This can be a more difficult stage of the resolution than it appears, especially if, as noted above, it is part of a communication with another. In agreeing the specifics of a solution which you have agreed to be generally workable, there is scope for further disagreement. If this starts to happen it is better to remind yourselves of the broad agreement briefly and your mutual desire to carry that through. It should be possible for you both to be close enough to the beneficial feeling of relief in achieving resolution to use the impetus of that to carry you over minor disagreements in working detail. It is not worth letting any discomfort at this stage create resolution-threatening delay. It is better to deal with small clashes at a time when you are both in a conciliatory frame of mind, having a mutual bond of working through to resolution of the issue.

You will have been through a highly charged emotional time in discussion to this point, which will have been positive overall in order to arrive at a solution, and you should now capitalise upon this in order to tie up the detailed working of the resolution. There will have been an understanding of the other's view and compromises on absolute starting positions. This will probably have arisen from some empathy for the other person's standpoint and a mutual feeling that a solution is worthwhile generally. So now, while this atmosphere prevails and all minds are on the same plane, is the best time to see the detail of the agreed way forward through to the end.

Be bold at this stage of resolution and try to bring your work and thoughts together to find a solution which feels right for you. Take action once you realise what needs to be done for your resolution. Remember that a resolution will be whatever it takes to eliminate conflict for you. If you can find ways to live with a situation and happily move forward with your life, it is effectively resolved! There are a few consolidation points for resolution, dealt with in the final chapter, which you should consider before conclusion of the resolution exercise.

CHAPTER 18

Beyond Resolution

"The reality today is that we are all interdependent and have to co-exist on this small planet. Therefore, the only sensible way of resolving differences and clashes of interests, whether between individuals or nations, is through dialogue"
The Dalai Lama

YOU MAY CONCLUDE THE conflict management process with a successfully reached and workable solution. In this case there will most likely be actions required to effect that solution, even if an agreement has been set or a plan recorded. Ensure that you follow through on the necessary steps needed by all involved to uphold a solution and make sure that agreed next steps and timescales are kept. I expand further on this below, as it is important to consolidate a resolution, maybe over some time, to prevent its evaporation.

Monitor Actions

Consolidation includes agreements with yourself and those with others - both on your side and theirs. Any agreements which you have decided can offer a resolution to a conflict could come to nothing if the effort is not put in to set them into motion and to monitor them. In the case of formal mediations, when an agreement is drawn up during a mediation, it will be lodged with any legal representatives who will know to follow-up, to ensure that the full benefit of the mediated solution is effected. Effort is required on a timely basis even in a formal setting, to ensure that an agreement takes effect and so it should be with your personal resolution and agreements. If momentum and input slacks at this point, much of the benefit of the whole exercise can be lost, even if there has been resolution and ensuing agreement. So be sure that once you know what your agreement looks like in practical terms and detail, you are certain to put it into action.

There may be further steps to be taken towards resolution after the exercise has been completed as far as possible by you, either before an agreement can be implemented or as part of it. This is also the case with some formal mediations and often agreed actions are required before resolution is achieved. If this is the case, you may feel that communication is now more freely flowing and that discussions can continue independently of the exercise which you have completed. If so, be sure to keep up the discussions, either verbal or written, in order to avoid the benefits of the exercise being diluted as time passes.

Touching base the next day to review steps for resolution or to follow-up on agreed actions is a good idea. Most formal mediations close with legal representatives agreeing to speak the next day. Even where there is a formal agreement with specified actions and timescales, this next day contact is still a good idea.

Agreement

As explained above an agreement should always be made as part of a resolution, however this is sometimes not possible, due to time or energy restraints. If all that is left incomplete at the conclusion of your exercise in conflict resolution is an actual note of agreement, ensure that this is completed as soon as possible. Alternatively, if you have not taken any advice, or employed help of another during the process, now may be the time to involve a formal or informal advisor or friend to ensure a good agreement or set way forward. As noted, it is not ideal to conclude a successful resolution conversation with a verbal agreement which has not been put into writing, but sometimes this situation can occur. If that is the case, do ensure that any agreement reached is recorded as soon as possible after the conversation and reviewed by parties to confirm an accurate and acceptable way forward. Leaving time for momentum to be lost, memory of conversation to lapse, or opportunity for old thought patterns to creep back is unhelpful and can sabotage much effort and progressive work to date.

In some cases of formal mediation good progress is made in the mediation, but an extended period of mediation is agreed to by all those present as being a worthwhile commitment. If that has been the conclusion of the mediation day, parties will already have or very shortly afterwards agree details of the date, time, and location of further mediation, because it is crucial to maintain the momentum of the work done within the mediation to date and the progress towards settlement which has been achieved.

If it is the case with your informal resolution process, that further discussion or thought would be helpful in achieving resolution, the same principles apply, and you should do what you can to take responsibility for driving forward promptly another conversation or more time for resolution. The more time which elapses between the last resolution session and the next, the greater the opportunity to lose both the memory of the actual progress to date and the attitudinal and relationship benefits gained so far.

No Conclusion

A communication or resolution exercise may have ended without an agreement, and it could be that further discussion may not have been arranged, but on reflection you may feel that further resolution work could lead to a successful agreement. Do think about this possibility and mention it to the other party. Sleeping on the issues raised can often produce a shift in attitude or approach which was not immediately forthcoming. This can yet lead to a successful mutual agreement after the event of an initial communication in many cases. For this reason, you should act on any thoughts of this sort quickly following the resolution exercise, rather than dismissing them, as the other party may slowly be shifting too.

If your resolution exercise has not concluded with an agreement and it seems that this is not possible or your own internal conflict cannot be resolved by your own work, do not despair of the conflict situation. It is very unlikely that nothing in the work you have done will benefit you. You will understand the situation better from many angles.

It is likely that if another is involved and there has been communication; views will have been expressed and points raised which will set the scene for further thought and a possible return to conciliatory discussion. Even if things have not extended as far as communication with another, your own understanding will have deepened and future resolution may stem from this.

Once seeds of new broader thought have been nurtured in yourself or another, a shift in the conflict area can gradually occur. Watch for this and give any movement in yourself or another the best chance of continuing to solution of the conflict. You will be well placed to do this following the work you have done to broaden thought and move away from a position towards needs and interests, with general aims in mind. If shifts in the conflict are noticed, consider returning to the relevant stages set out; take the opportunity to think again or communicate openly with another. There might be thought behind the scenes on what has been said and taken into consideration up until now. A little further work, if the opening arises, might be just what is needed to complete resolution. It may be that resolution will flow organically from what has been said and done as part of this exercise.

In any case the work that has been done will be positive. It will help current and future conflicts in your life. You should now be more aware of the process and how to deal with conflicts, having reinforced the beneficial concept that any conflict is negative in our lives and the stress it creates is worth eliminating. You will have gained an understanding of how to examine the elements of a conflict and you will be armed with the ability to move from a position on an issue towards interests and needs, which yield resolution ideas. You will have given time to developing your own perception of thought, feelings, decision-making and communication in relation to resolution.

Conflict should always be identified, worked with, and understood in order to resolve it or to do the utmost to come to terms with the elements involved in it. This process gives us back some control over things which are a way we do not wish them to be. With that control and understanding, stress levels are reduced. Conflict is eliminated or reduced to the extent that aims and needs within the conflict area, and in life generally, take the precedence that they require for life to move forward in the direction you wish it to.

Conclusion

I HOPE YOU HAVE worked through the stages in this book and completed the individual input required for you to reach realisations and conclusions which represent a resolution to your own specific conflict. A resolution will usually be found in some mix of deeper understanding, satisfaction, compromise, and acceptance. The proportions of each of these or an alternative solution which suits, will be specific to you.

If you have worked through this book, you will have reached a stage where the problem feels less stressful to you. It is helpful to really tap into how the issue makes you feel after this work. Take a moment to close your eyes and consider how you feel compared to how you felt at the beginning of the exercise. Have you fully considered the issues and the realisation of possible solutions? I hope this has made a real difference to the feelings you get when you consider the problem.

The tools I have shared should have given you the opportunity to gain a deeper understanding of the conflict and of yourself in relation to it. I have shown you how to look at various solutions and their individual value to you. I hope this has enabled you to select and apply the right solutions for you, to your specific conflict.

To resolve a conflict, you need to gain valuable understanding of and insights into the specific conflict worked upon, which these exercises will have helped with. Whatever conclusions to resolution which you have reached or gained insights into, you can be sure that these solutions have come from you, rather than being imposed upon you and that you have applied many individual factors relevant specifically to you. Therefore, you can guarantee that your conclusions will be tailored to you.

From this process, I hope that you will have found more harmony in your current life. I hope too that you have found ways to deal well with future conflicts. Although each conflict is different and requires new work, you will now be familiar with the tools employed to resolve conflicts. You will also know how these tools work for you and understand your own best approach to resolution.

Although you cannot always choose your problems, you can at least choose the way in which you deal with them and a way of resolving them which is acceptable to you. In addition to dealing with conflicts and feeling the increased harmony which that brings, I hope that you have learned from and enjoyed the process of conflict resolution for your life and that it stays with you.

About the Author

GEORGIA LAY LIVES IN the South West of England with her husband. They have three sons, now all adults.

She began her career in finance, working for one of the big four international accountancy firms where she qualified as a Chartered Accountant and worked in that field for a decade. Georgia worked from home and took on voluntary positions during her childrens' pre-school years. When her youngest son started playgroup, she re-qualified as a Barrister, and went on to run her own successful Civil and Commercial practice.

Fairly suddenly and very unexpectedly Georgia was diagnosed with Multiple Sclerosis, with which it became increasingly difficult to find the energy for a busy work and private life. Georgia spent the next few years consolidating on her long-held love of yoga, which she taught on a voluntary basis for a while before returning to law to qualify in Mediation. Georgia found with this, a professional thinking which came into line with the personal ethos she has developed.

Although there was a time when the win at court had been her driving force, mediation now makes perfect sense.

She has become passionate about the avoidance of conflict and how resolution of issues can help people in so many ways with the harmonious progression of life.

You can find more about Georgia on her social media channels:-

Linkedin:
https://www.linkedin.com/in/georgia-lay-34739725/

Instagram: Resolvetheconflict

Tik Tok: Resolvetheconflict